Behold
the Harvest

by Dale Rumble

Revival Press
An Imprint of
Destiny Image® Publishers, Inc.
P.O. Box 310
Shippensburg, PA 17257-0310

ISBN 1-56043-192-X

For Worldwide Distribution
Printed in the U.S.A.

First Printing: 1998   Second Printing: 1998

This book and all other Destiny Image, Revival Press,
and Treasure House books are available
at Christian bookstores and distributors worldwide.

For a U.S. bookstore nearest you, call **1-800-722-6774**.
For more information on foreign distributors,
call **717-532-3040**.
Or reach us on the Internet: **http://www.reapernet.com**

Acknowledgments

I wish to express special thanks to Claudia Scott (Scott Info-Tech) for her significant contribution in typing, creating graphics and formatting the manuscript, as well as for her gracious advice and counsel.

I also thank those who critiqued preliminary drafts of the text. In particular I thank my son, Donald, for his review, suggestions, and insight.

Finally, I thank Bertha, my dear wife and partner in ministry, for her prayers, patience, and encouragement that enabled me to write.

Endorsements

"Dale Rumble is a man whose deep love for Jesus and long-term record of integrity are apparent through the insights in his book. He loves the Church and has sought the Lord for years to know the times and seasons for the Church. His wisdom has been a source of refreshing to many in the Body of Christ."

— Mike Bickle, Pastor, Metro Christian Fellowship, Kansas City, Kansas

"I found Dale Rumble's book to be stimulating in thought. His analysis of what is on God's agenda for the Church is on the cutting edge of subjects to which all thinking pastors must give due consideration. His passion for the harvest is obvious and the chart at the beginning of the book on the population explosion is powerful. I enjoyed the book and believe it to be part of a growing body of literature pertaining to the subject of the harvest and the role of apostles and prophets in the harvest."

— Randy Clark, St. Louis, Missouri

"*Behold the Harvest* is, of course, an excellent appraisal of the significance of the current awakening in the context of God's ultimate purpose for the Church, and it is particularly commendable for the way that it weaves important practical considerations into the discussion of these matters. I do appreciate Dale's insight into God's plan for humanity and for the Church, and I like very much the way that Dale has interwoven practical considerations into his discussion, highlighting the importance of such things as humility in attaining to all that God has for us."

— Richard Riss, Zarephath Bible Institute, Piscataway, New Jersey

"*Behold the Harvest* provides a clear, prophetic aerial view of what our awesome God is up to in this 'day of visitation' and beckons us to fully enter in with confidence and joy. Fasten your seatbelt. We are in for quite a ride!"

— Jerry Steingard, Pastor, Jubilee Christian Fellowship, Stratford, Ontario

"After reading *Behold the Harvest*, I was struck by how timely this word is for preparing the Body of Christ for the coming harvest. God has given Dale insight into the needs of churches and Christian workers in this present hour. Dale's book will contribute to raising up "Barns" and "Reapers" at this, the threshold of the new millennium. I found the chapter, "Glory of His Presence," with the various Greek words describing our progress into spiritual adulthood, to be extremely helpful. I could only wish that each new convert *and* each one who is discipler of others would benefit from reading this book."

"Dale has once again spoken from the heart of God with a fresh word for God's people in this 'time and season.' For all those who desire to understand and flow with the current renewal and coming great harvest of souls, this book is a must-read. Dale has captured the essence of this current renewal (revival) and placed it in both biblical and historical context; then liberally added much personal wisdom gleaned from more than 40 years in the ministry. A must-read!"

Table of Contents

Preface

Why am I writing this book? Because something very important is beginning to take place!

Report after report speaks of a sovereign dawn of "Sonshine" upon the Church. Some examples are the growing number of men in the Promise Keepers movement who are embracing their God-given responsibilities as fathers and husbands, the spontaneous growth of the March For Jesus that unites the churches in their witness for Christ, the increased emphasis of intercessory prayer, and the numerous locations worldwide where large numbers of souls are coming to Christ.

More dramatic phenomena are the reports of sovereign outpourings of God's love and grace, where great joy, laughing, dancing, weeping, shaking, prophetic words, and visions mark a divine visitation. Crippling bondages (many demonic) are broken in lives by God's anointing. When His life is received it is quickly imparted to others so that the "fire" of the Holy Spirit is spread quickly. "Catch the fire" has become a common expression of what is taking place in cities, regions, and nations. Conviction of sin, repentance, and reconciliation see backsliders and marriages restored; prophetic revelations in word and worship express His heart. And His message is simple, "I *love* you; and I want you, My bride, to passionately respond to Me in this hour." Who does He love? Everyone— adults and children, shepherds and sheep.

One thing becomes clear when the fruits and manifestations of this visitation are considered: The sovereignty of how God moves transcends our human reasoning and traditions. He will not stay confined in the box of our theology! There are no denominational boundaries to His love.

To me, one of the greatest realities of God's presence is to see the joy and dancing of the children; how they are so easily touched by His anointing.

I have become much more aware of how much He loves me, *just as I am.* This awareness brings a greater sense of intimacy. To some, the result is an infectious spread of joy; to others it is weeping and intercession. Most importantly, hearts are changed.

What is taking place is not some transient flash of religious fervor. It is a divine window of opportunity that God has opened for the Church to enter into His purpose for this generation.

A telescope can only give the viewer a clear picture of what it is focused on; if the focus is on a wrong object, the resulting image can mislead the viewer. Our spiritual telescope must be focused on the heart of God. What is His strategy for the days that lie ahead?

That is what this book is all about.

From eternity He has known all that He will accomplish in this period of time. Everything is on schedule. We must know that all things are in His hands and under His control, and that He will accomplish His purpose!

> *...I am God, and there is no other; I am God, and there is no one like Me, declaring the end from the beginning and from ancient times things which have not been done, saying, "My purpose will be established, and I will accomplish all My good pleasure"* (Isaiah 46:9-10).

Introduction

Jesus challenged the Pharisees and Sadducees of His day with a question that is pertinent to us today (see Mt. 16:1-3):

Do you know how to discern the appearance of the sky, but cannot discern the signs of the times?

He wept over the city of Jerusalem knowing that she would shortly be destroyed by the Romans simply because she had not recognized the day of her visitation (see Lk. 19:42-44).

How sad for the nation of Israel, but how much more so for us, if we, upon whom the end of the ages has come, fail to recognize our day of visitation!

God made man in His image; He created us to be loved and with the capability of responding to His love. He loved the world enough to send His only Son to die sacrificially in our place. He paid the ultimate price to redeem us. There is no force in existence greater than the love of God; because of His love, God is beginning to renew the Church.

A refreshing breeze of the Holy Spirit blowing over the earth is destined to become a mighty wind as the purpose of God unfolds. He is visiting His people again. Multitudes are turning to Christ. New songs of the Spirit are coming forth in worship; new dimensions of joy fill many hearts. Laughter abounds!

It appears that a great renewal is beginning, preparing our hearts for what lies ahead. I do not believe in setting dates for the Lord's return, but I am persuaded that He is arising as Lord of the harvest to begin a glorious end-time work in the earth. The nations are in His hands and His sovereignty reigns over all (see Ps. 22:28; 103:19). A great harvest lies ahead, one that could be the end of this age!

The final harvest could take place over an extended period of time and involve our children or even their children. I do not know whether we are now entering that glorious finale or simply another revival. However, we face *significant* challenges if this visitation does lead into the last harvest. For that reason, we should understand the implications and prepare our hearts accordingly.

The Lord will do nothing without revealing it to His servants the prophets (see Amos 3:7). In recent years, there has been an increasing number of visions and prophetic messages calling the Church to prepare for what lies ahead; to turn from going our own way, to give Him all of our hearts, and to rest in His love. He is all we will ever need!

It appears to me that when the Holy Spirit falls upon the Church as refreshing rain, everyone is happy. However, when He comes as wind, some believers become alarmed as

God begins to shake things in His house that are not of Him. And when the Holy Spirit comes as fire, those who are unwilling to be purged head for the hills! Believers who recognize their need and humble themselves will find new purity and power in their relationship with the Lord. The truth is that all three works of the Holy Spirit (refreshing, shaking, and purging) are necessary for genuine revival in the Church. The Lord wants *all* of our hearts. Sin and holiness must become realities. And renewal is the divine process by which this takes place.

I believe the gospel will yet have a much greater impact on nations than in any previous revival. At the same time, the bride of Christ will be prepared for her Lord, becoming a victorious, overcoming Church clothed with the glory of God! And all this in a time of deepening darkness in the world.

My vision and expectations of these events, which are beginning to come to pass, are the theme of this book.

Chapter 1

The Birth of Renewal

Where Are We Today?

This is an important question. Do we expect the future to be a continuation of what has been taking place, or are we entering a time of great change? What lies ahead? These questions are in the hearts of many believers, and there are answers!

The place to begin is recognizing how vitally important and precious to God are the souls of men. The earth's population grew from around 400 million in AD 500 to approximately 800 million in the mid-1700's. In other words, it doubled in roughly 1,250 years. Now it doubles in less than one hundred years.

1

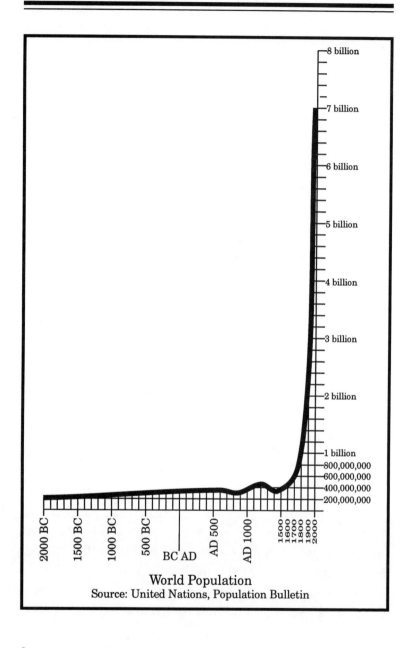

World Population
Source: United Nations, Population Bulletin

The preceding graph of world population growth dramatically illustrates the potential harvest that exists. In the last century of this millennium, the population is expected to be 7 billion, and reach 8.6 billion by the year 2025. The astronomical number and rate of increase of souls living on the earth point to our day as a time ripe for a visitation of God. Christ died for each individual, and for the first time, His anointing and supporting technology make it possible for every soul to hear the gospel in their lifetime. This is a picture of the harvest fields that God sees. We are living at a unique time in history!

There are three streams of events that characterize this period of history.

1. The first stream is the rapidly growing darkness and spiritual deception in the world. Although this is true for all nations, it is a great shame and reproach for America because of her Christian heritage. She once esteemed the laws of God in her courts and schools, but now she has removed them from her social conscience. As a consequence we are a country that is spiritually crippled by sins of the occult, humanism, abortion, homosexuality, pornography, child abuse, drug addiction, and gang violence. There is a spirit of lawlessness in the streets. Satanism is increasing, and more powerful mind-altering drugs are appearing in the marketplace. As a result of these sins there is a large and growing number of dysfunctional and homeless people in our cities.

As a nation, we have begun to call evil good, and good evil. Homosexuality is now approved as a valid lifestyle. Over 33 million unborn babies have been killed in America since the Supreme Court's decision to legalize abortion. Freedom of choice and permissive lifestyles that include perversion are legally protected rather than moral conduct based on God's laws. Social goals are based on a spirit of materialism that has created enormous personal and governmental debt. Murder rates are the highest among developed nations. God has been taken out of our schools and courts. Drug use is rampant among the youth of our nation. Children bring guns to school; gang violence is common in city streets. Pornographic movies and videos are readily available in the marketplace. The rates of divorce and rape are high and increasing. Education programs in schools endorse the use of condoms and make them available to the children. Instead of teaching the principles of righteousness, New Age concepts and practices are promoted.

2. The second stream of events is the exponential advance of discovery in various fields of science. Daniel prophesied of this increase in knowledge (see Dan. 12:4). Some pertinent examples are: genetic engineering; semiconductor technology with the corresponding fall-out of inexpensive, high-power computers; space technology; communication and video technologies, including the "Internet"; nuclear and biological weapon systems. Over 80% of all scientists who ever lived are alive today, and their capability is greatly increased because of highly advanced tools and facilities.

Satan uses science to turn men away from God, and to take lives on a massive scale in wars and terrorism. God, on the other hand, can use science to send His gospel into all areas of the world!

3. The third stream of events is by far the most important. It is God's strategy, the plans of His heart, to visit the earth and gather in a great and final harvest. Our God

is a consuming fire, and His strategy is twofold: to call men and nations to repentance through the fire of His judgments; and to renew and purify the Church with the fire of the Holy Spirit.

In his book, *The Gates of Hell Shall Not Prevail*, Dr. D. James Kennedy presents figures from author and church statistician Dr. David Barrett that show there is an accelerating numerical growth of evangelical Christians in the world; the approximate ratio of evangelical believers to world population was:

1 in 99 by 1430
1 in 49 by 1790
1 in 19 by 1970
1 in 9 by 1993

This encouraging trend is the leading edge of a great wave of harvest which we will consider in the following pages.

The Fire of Judgment

How did America, as a "Christian" nation, lose the way of righteousness? A country that tolerates or endorses sins, such as abortion, will not recognize when it crosses the threshold of God's patience by transgressions which bring His judgment upon the land.

The principles of justice in the Law of God, like Himself, do not change. During the Old Testament, when Israel backslid from serving the Lord and went into idolatry, He sent judgments that He had forewarned them of. These judgments consisted of pestilence, crop failures by insects and droughts, wars, captivity, and natural calamities such as earthquakes, famines, violent winds, hailstones, etc. (see 2 Chron. 7:13-14; Ezekial 13:10-13; Amos 4:6-10). God's moral absolutes have not changed, so why should His judgment of national transgressions be any different?

Fire purifies as well as destroys. And this is what we face in our nation today. God is speaking to America through shakings that He is bringing upon the land. It is important to recognize that floods, AIDS, anarchy in our streets, economic problems, earthquakes, wars, riots, ethnic strife, hurricanes, etc., are the fire of God! They are instruments through which He speaks to us, and they are wholly under His control. Even though calamities arise because of sin, they never take place apart from God's sovereignty. His judgments are redemptive in their intent, for they are blended with mercy. Their purpose is to call our nation to repentance. God allows the consequences of our sins to become a curse that is intended to move us toward humility and repentance. To we who are Christians, these winds of calamity and adversity are not sent to destroy us, but to deepen our roots in Him and to bring us into His purpose for the nation. The important subject of God's judgments has been addressed in an excellent book by Clay Sterrett.[1]

God calls us to intercede for our country by personally identifying with her sins so that we come before God as repentant representatives. We are to humble ourselves in fasting and prayer just as Daniel prayed for his people, Israel (see Dan. 9:3-19). This means to seek forgiveness for sins such as abortion, homosexuality, etc., and to pray for a spirit of supplication and repentance to sweep the land.

The Fire of Renewal

The following reports are evidence of a divine wind of renewal and revival that has been increasing in intensity as it has blown over the earth in recent years. It appears destined to become an international visitation of the Holy Spirit that will impact every nation on earth, for that is the scope of God's kingdom.

In 1990, Dr. Peter Wagner, professor of church growth at Fuller Theological Seminary, reported in an article in *Ministries Today* that there were 78,000 new converts every day. He stated that the number of Christians in Africa is expected to reach 324 million by the year 2000.

In describing the phenomenal growth of the underground church in Communist China, Arthur Wallis[2] wrote that in 1983 there were probably over 50 million believers in that nation, which has the largest population of any country in the world. There are many more today. Unconfirmed reports estimate that 35,000 persons are saved every day.

In March of 1995, the gospel was broadcast in a large cooperative program from Puerto Rico to 165 nations. The potential listening audience was one billion people. (There is a special place in my heart for this medium. In 1951, I was saved through the radio ministry of Charles Fuller).

There is a growing global movement of intercessory prayer. Intercessors for America and Intercessors for Canada are examples. Much prayer focus targets a geographic region of the world located between 10° and 40° north (latitude) of the equator known as the *10/40 Window*. This region is homeland for over 70% of all unreached peoples and for most of the world's poverty. In October of 1995, 30 million Christians prayed for the salvation of 100 strategic cities in this window.

In April of 1996, the "Billy Graham World Television Series" broadcast the gospel to 200 countries. One million churches, from every continent, worked to mobilize "home television gatherings" to view the gospel presentation. The potential audience was 2.5 billion persons.

The August 1996 issue of *March for Jesus USA* reports that in 1996 between 10 and 12 million people worldwide marched for Jesus in over 2,000 cities of 170 nations. The largest march in the world was at Sao Paulo, Brazil, where an estimated 1.5 million people took part. What a testimony of renewal!

In October 1997, a dramatic testimony of what renewal is all about was made to the leaders and people of this nation (America). Approximately 1 million Promise Keepers assembled at the Monument Mall in Washington D.C. to publicly commit themselves, with repentance, to be godly husbands and fathers; men who will stand against racism and sectarianism in the body of Christ. Church renewal begins in the home!

Seven of the 10 largest churches in the world are in South Korea. There are over 4 million believers in the capital city of Seoul. Most church leaders in that land believe God has placed a special call on their nation to proclaim the gospel of Christ. By 1992 they had sent between 2,000 and 3,000 missionaries to other lands, and they plan to increase that number to 10,000 by the end of this century. Their churches are known for a commitment to prayer, often in the early morning.

The June 1996 edition of *Charisma* magazine carries a report on the evangelical revival that is sweeping the nations of Latin America. The article states that 400 people an hour are being converted to Christ. During the last decade, Protestant believers have increased from 18.6 million to 59.4 million, which is 9 times the population growth! The Assemblies of God in Brazil have grown tenfold since 1980 to 15 million members in 90,000 local assembles. In Peru, a Protestant church is planted every 8 hours. There are many revival centers in these countries; the largest of which is Ekklesia, an independent charismatic church with 11,000 members in La Paz, Bolivia. Evangelism has been undergirded with selfless sacrifice in prayer and spiritual warfare. This move of the Holy Spirit is marked by new dimensions of spontaneous worship. Much of the revival momentum is coming from young people. While Argentina has a long history of revival, there are reports of a greater anointing coming to churches in that nation. God is on the move in South America!

Since January 20, 1994, what is now known as the Toronto Airport Christian Fellowship became the center of a tremendous renewal move of the Holy Spirit in Canada. Senior Pastor John Arnott and his wife Carol had prayed much for revival. Their prayers were answered when visiting minister Randy Clark, Pastor of the Vineyard Christian Fellowship in St. Louis, began meetings at the church. God has so moved that the outpouring which began then has become international in impact. People have been coming to the meetings from nations in Asia, Europe, Islands of the Sea, South America, and Africa, as well as the United States, Australia, New Zealand, and Russia. In the first 30 months, a cumulative total of well over one million persons have attended. The United Kingdom has been significantly impacted as roughly 9,000 congregations (4,000 of them Anglican churches) have been touched by the "Toronto Blessing." Pentecostal churches in the U.K. have initiated their largest ever church planting program, and Baptist churches there plan to plant 2,000 new churches by the end of this century. The Toronto meetings are marked by supernatural experiences of a manifest presence of the Holy Spirit. Joy, shaking, being drunk in the Spirit, freedom, and healing are common, plus a new consciousness of the love of God! Sinners are saved and "prodigals" return home. There is a strong prophetic content in ministry calling God's people to worship and intercession. Denominational barriers disappear as believers from many streams flow together in the joy of what the Lord is doing in their midst. The spirit of unity is exemplified by the men and women working together in the ministry teams as they pray for the many visitors. These precious people, as well as those on the worship teams, come from a number of churches of different denominations in the Toronto and southern Ontario region.

America has been touched by a revival that came to Pensacola, Florida, on June 18, 1995. Pastor John Kilpatrick of the Brownsville Assembly of God had been praying for revival for over two years. When visiting evangelist Steve Hill began to preach that June day, the Holy Spirit fell in awesome power. Souls were saved and the meetings continue to the present. Dr. Michael Brown, who has joined the church teaching staff, makes the following three observations on this revival in the October 1996 issue of his *I.C.N. Ministries* Newsletter.

> "More than 45,000 sinners and backsliders have surrendered their lives to God from a total cumulative attendance of over 1 million people since the meetings began. Crime rate in the county has dropped over 17%.

> "The presence of God in meetings has been manifest. When evangelist Hill is preaching, conviction has been so strong that some sinners have fallen out of the pews and need help to come forward to the altar; others have literally ran to the altar. The preaching has been uncompromising messages of repentance, holiness and God's love.

"People line up as early as 8 am to find seats in the 7 pm services, with an overflow of 6,000 being common. They come from various states as well as other nations with 400-500 leaders attending each week, often going back to see revival break out in their home church."

Manifestations often occur when individuals are moved upon by the Holy Spirit. Denominational walls come down as believers from many streams flow together in what the Lord is doing. His sovereignty is very evident in what is taking place at Pensacola. And it has begun to spread to other cities!

There are other churches and ministries in various places, besides the ones mentioned here, where there is renewal. The common thread of each is God's sovereign anointing on vessels who humble themselves in prayer and intercession for the harvest—men and women who know that the message of the cross is the power of God.

A question that arises concerns the Catholic Church. This denomination was touched by the Charismatic movement; is it open to renewal today?

What About the Catholics?

There are apparently over 300,000 charismatic Catholics worldwide. Is the spirit of renewal moving in their midst? The following two reports from India and Mexico help to answer this question.

Evangelist Matthew Naikomparambil is a charismatic Catholic priest in Kerala, India. The story of his ministry is recorded in the November 1994 edition of *Charisma*. Father Matthew was baptized in the Spirit nearly 30 years ago. Since then he has become known for his huge evangelistic campaigns that rely on "signs and wonders." There have been

11

many miracles of healing take place when he prays for the sick. He is referred to as the "Billy Graham of India," and has ministered throughout India and Nepal. His Divine Retreat Centre draws thousands of visitors a week. There is a staff of over 200 who intercede for the center's work. He prays from 3:00 a.m. to 6:00 a.m. daily and continues to pray in tongues during the day.

The October 1996 issue of *Spread the Fire*, a renewal networking magazine published by the Toronto Airport Christian Fellowship, contains the following remarkable account from Mexico.

"Revival is happening in Mexico within the Catholic church reports Wesley Campbell, senior pastor of the New Life Vineyard, Kelowna, British Columbia. Campbell visited Mexico City and Juarez in the summer of 1996 with John Arnott and a ministry team.

"Through Victor Richards, a Juarez pastor who had visited Toronto, Campbell discovered the mountain retreat of Father Hilberto Gomez where he witnessed 70,000 Mexicans come from across the country in trucks and buses on a single weekend to hear the gospel preached and to receive prayer. Campbell believes he has witnessed a revival within the Catholic church the magnitude of that experienced by great reformers such as Luther and Wesley. I heard Gomez say, 'The idols cannot save you; Mary cannot save you; unless a man is born again he cannot see the kingdom of God.'

"When Gomez gave an altar call, 10,000 came forward to renounce their sins and accept Jesus as their Savior. Hundreds of sick were brought on pallets, stretchers and wheelchairs, and others lined up for prayer. 'I have pictures of Father Hilberto with arms full of crutches as people have been healed of every type of disease,' states Campbell. 'When the power of the Holy Spirit touched them, they fell, shook, trembled and were filled with the Holy Spirit.'

"As groups of pilgrims arrive, they are ushered onto fields and lined up. Catholic evangelists walk along the lines preaching the gospel to each new group and praying for each one.

"Gomez was baptized in the Holy Spirit 15 years ago when another priest said to him, "Father Hilberto, God loves you." The Spirit of God came upon him so powerfully that for an entire year he wept whenever he thought of the Lord.

"According to Campbell, Gomez had previously struggled as a priest for 28 years, but after being filled with Spirit said, 'I was a priest in darkness. Even in all my masses, I didn't know the Lord Jesus.'

"Seven years ago Gomez was offered a 100 acre villa in the mountains. Since then hundreds of thousands have made their way to the villa. He has trained 2,500 lay preachers who oversee about 10,000 prayer groups of born-again believers throughout Mexico."

While these statistics look good, they fall far short of what is in the heart of God for the future. Multitudes have not heard the gospel, while the population of the earth is exploding! Over 3,000 ethnic language groups have yet to hear the gospel for the first time.

The prophet Isaiah describes a time when darkness will cover the earth and deep darkness the peoples. At that time the glory of God will arise upon the church and draw nations to her light (see Is. 60:1-7). The darkness is already here, but where is the glory? That is the issue facing the Church today.

Renewal is a divine prelude to revival, preparing the Church for the glory by which multitudes will be saved. The Church is not ready for the darkness while the glory is missing. It is not a matter of resources, methodology, doctrine, or even zeal. What is needed is a deep work in hearts to prepare His people with the mercy and compassion to release God's love to the world. To have the glory of God is to have His love, power, and passion for the lost. This can only come out of a deep intimate relationship with Him. That is what renewal is all about!

We Experience the Fire

In the spring of 1994, some of us who were in local church oversight began to hear reports of renewal that were accompanied with strange manifestations. Reports of the spectacular always spread quickly. The phenomenon included weeping, unrestrained laughter, trembling, falling "under the power of God" and being "drunk" in the Spirit.

What was taking place? This became the question that led us to the renewal in Toronto. What we discovered, to put it simply, was *Father blessing His children!* We would never be the same again.

I personally had experienced God's blessings in the "Latter Rain" and "Charismatic" renewals. The former, while more limited in its impact on the Church overall, did experience anointed worship with new spiritual songs of promised restoration. God often moved sovereignly in prophecy, with the laying on of hands, to confirm the call of individuals to ministry. Indeed, that was how the Lord called my wife, Bertha, and myself to begin our ministry. On the other hand, the Charismatic renewal was much more widespread, bringing reality of baptism in the Spirit to multitudes, in particular, to non-Pentecostal bodies of believers. The emerging of spiritual gifts created a fresh vision of body life for many. At this time, our church experienced for the first time, the life, love, and bonds of fellowship we had long envisioned and sought to build. We oriented meetings around meals together, teaching, and body ministry where members were encouraged to participate through prayer, testimony, and spiritual gifts. Freedom, spontaneity, and joyful worship were highlights of gatherings, and souls were saved.

Both of these renewals were refreshing rains of God's Spirit.

But *this* renewal is different! The emphasis is not primarily new truth, but on bringing the reality of existing truth deeper into our hearts; especially in the area of our relationship with Him and with one another. I have personally been convicted of my need for greater humility and a deeper prayer life. In effect, the Lord is dealing with those things that hinder His glory. A key focus is how much He loves us and how greatly He seeks our response to His love.[3] The Holy Spirit is removing veils of complacency, apathy, pride, prayerlessness, control, etc., from hearts, things which keep us from intimacy with our Father in Heaven. Intimacy requires an honest and willing opening up of our hearts to Him—inner secrets, needs, desires, apprehensions, insecurities—things which He already knows about, but which He wants us to bring to Him as our Father.

A common thread of renewal testimonies concerns sins and idols being revealed and put away. Since our church has embraced renewal, we have seen lives changed, broken relationships healed, and backsliders restored. The fruit is good!

A great help and blessing has been anointed worship songs in the Spirit which express the joy and reality of His love for us. In all of this, He is calling us to greater commitment to the way of His cross. However, the greatest impact for good has been revelation that our prayer life was woefully inadequate for the call God had placed upon us as a church. We in leadership have had to repent for an emphasis on intercession and prayer that was more geared to maintenance mode than to an aggressive warfare necessary for a great harvest of souls. The history of church revivals makes it abundantly clear how vital prayer and fasting have always been, and will continue to be, in the purpose of God.

The January 1997 issue of *Charisma* reports a conference on prayer and fasting:

> "Concerned that the United States may be teetering on the brink of God's judgment, about 3,700 Christians met in St. Louis in mid-November for a three-day session of fasting and prayer that focused on the nation's need for spiritual revival. Some participants wept openly as they knelt in small groups and repented for their own sins and for the sins of the American church.
>
> " 'This meeting is a matter of great urgency. It is a matter of life and earth,' announced Bill Bright, founder of Campus Crusade for Christ and chief organizer of the conference. He and other ministry leaders representing a broad coalition of church groups led the mostly white audience in repentance for racism, denominationalism and the country's moral decline."

This is one of many examples of a renewed interest in fasting that is beginning to sweep the churches who are moving in renewal.

Furthermore, renewal is only beginning! Greater demonstrations of God's fire will be seen in the days ahead. He will deal with pride and sectarian attitudes, for humility is essential if the glory of God is to arise on the Church! We are not to fear the fire of God, for our hearts must be purged and prepared for what lies ahead.

Many in the harvest will come from the poor, afflicted, and handicapped, from our streets, from Islamic nations, from Asian and African nations, from lands crippled by Communism. There will also be many in Israel who find their Messiah. All will respond to a gospel that demonstrates the love, mercy, and compassion of God, and exhibits the power of the Holy Spirit.

The harvest will be the final great revelation of God's love, mercy, and grace before the coming of His terrible day of wrath (see 1 Pet. 1:13).

The Anointing

How are we to understand and judge the impact of God's anointing on human faculties? Unusual displays of what takes place are spoken of as "manifestations." These are certainly biblical (see Dan. 10:7-11,15-17; Jer. 23:9; Acts 2:1-21; 2 Cor. 12:2; Rev. 1:7). Although biblical, they have no value in themselves. The following are guidelines of wisdom and safety in shepherding spiritual experiences:

❖ We are to seek the Lord; we are *not* to seek for signs.

❖ Believers, and leaders in particular, are to judge the validity of what takes place by the fruit that follows, not by any sign or manifestation. Transformation of hearts is the only credible proof of renewal.

What is often referred to as a manifestation of the Spirit is, in fact, generally the human reaction of a believer's

17

psychological makeup to a strong presence of the Holy Spirit. While the Holy Spirit can move in such a way as to give a sign, it is also true that a deep work can be done in hearts without any apparent manifestation.[4] The historical record of the great revivals in the 18th and 19th centuries is filled with accounts of many signs similar to those being experienced today. The fruit that resulted from these visitations of the Holy Spirit suggests that a very deep work done in hearts was responsible for what took place.

The end result of anointings of the Holy Spirit can be understood and explained by the anointing that rested upon Jesus as the Christ. He received the Spirit without measure for specific ministry goals which provide a basis for judging the fruit of anointed ministry.

Let us examine each one as they are listed in Isaiah 61:1-3:

- ❖ To bring good news to the afflicted.

- ❖ To bind up the brokenhearted.

- ❖ To proclaim liberty to captives and freedom to prisoners.

- ❖ To proclaim the favorable year of the Lord and the day of vengeance of our God.

- ❖ To comfort all who mourn.

- ❖ To grant those who mourn in Zion, giving them a garland instead of ashes, the oil of gladness instead of mourning, the mantle of praise instead of a spirit of fainting.

- ❖ The goal of all this ministry is for God's people to become oaks of righteousness, the planting of the Lord, who glorify Him.

Thus, the validity of any revival, as a genuine visitation of God, can be determined by the absence or presence of the following:

❖ The gospel will be proclaimed and people warned to flee from the day of God's vengeance and wrath.

❖ What God purposes to do in His visitation will be made known. Thus, prophetic revelations and visions should be expected.

❖ Love, mercy, compassion, and comfort will be ministered to those who are emotionally and spiritually crippled.

❖ Deliverance will be ministered to those held captive by spiritual depression or oppression, the occult, other hidden works of darkness (i.e. sickness, unforgiveness, pride, deception, fear, lust of the flesh, etc.).

❖ God's people will be set free from hindrances to prayer, worship, praise, and rejoicing. It is significant that the anointing upon Jesus, described in Isaiah 61:1-3, has more references to replacing mourning and fainting with gladness and praise than any other activity. Joy is an important sign of renewed life.

❖ Believers will become rooted in Christ, not as reeds or willows, but as oaks of righteousness who will not be tossed about by circumstances and every wind of doctrine.

When spiritual experiences are outside the experiential comfort zone or theological boundaries of Christians, they may discount what is taking place, ascribing it to emotions, bad theology, or even demonic deception. While we must judge any manifestation by the fruit that follows, the real issue is often simply one of heart attitude.

During the Pentecostal revival in the early days of this century, many Evangelical Christians discredited what was taking place and referred to Spirit-filled believers as "holy rollers." Physical and spiritual manifestations, including spiritual gifts, became cerebral stumbling blocks that exposed the heart of these critics. The real issue was their heart attitude more than correct theology.

We think, reason and make decisions in the natural world by our rational minds. However, our mental faculties alone are not sufficient in the kingdom of God. For this reason, the Lord gives us an anointing of His Spirit to teach and guide us in His ways, which will often be in conflict with our rational minds (see Rm. 8:14).

And as for you, the anointing which you received from Him abides in you, and you have no need for anyone to teach you; but as His anointing teaches you about all things, and is true and is not a lie, and just as it has taught you, you abide in Him (1 John 2:27).

It is imperative to guard our hearts so that we will walk under His anointing rather than by natural reasoning, especially in these days of renewal and restoration.

Confidence in what we can accomplish by traditional, controlled, predictable, "business-as-usual" meetings has to be replaced by humble recognition that only the anointing of God will be sufficient for the task that lies ahead. Historically, any new move of the Holy Spirit has generally been marked by spontaneity and originality.

In 1994, when I first visited the church in Toronto that God had raised up as a renewal center, I was attracted by the humility of those in charge. There was no exaltation of manifestations, of leaders, or their denomination; only Jesus was lifted up. The gentle authority of servanthood was evident in the ministry and oversight of meetings. I could not deny the truth and reality of what I saw. To a large extent, we were committed to embrace what God was doing by what we saw in these leaders.

Finally, true renewal does not require one to have any outward manifestations; a deep work in hearts can be marked by quiet brokenness and repentance. The primary essence of true renewal is simply Jesus coming into His rightful place in hearts. The long-range fruit of renewal is not a series of experiences; it is a new, continual lifestyle that reflects the heart and purpose of God. However it does come, we need renewal!

Where Do We Go From Here?

If we are entering the final visitation of God that concludes in the great end-time harvest, then the following are challenges to be faced:

❖ Although not intentionally, some bodies of believers have confined God inside the box of their theological understanding. As a consequence, they can fail to see or understand the significance of His visitation; they may not see their own lack or the seriousness of these days. Wrong eschatology can limit how well we recognize and embrace the purpose of God.

❖ It is important that leaders do not hinder, control, or institutionalize what the Spirit is doing. It is the Lord's purpose, not our agendas, that is important.

❖ Our emphasis in doctrine needs to be reassessed. All truth is important. However, many of the truths that we emphasize pale in significance when compared to the emphasis Jesus places on unity in His body. One purpose of His anointing is to bring into being the answer to His prayer—that all believers become one functioning body in Him (see Jn. 17:21-23). Unity cannot come apart from forgiveness and reconciliation across denominational, racial, and ethnic boundaries. There is no option for walls of division in the body of Christ.

✤ As His servants, we need to readjust our criteria for success. Excellence in what we do is not the proper emphasis. The work ahead is something that only the Lord can do. We ought to be totally concerned with guarding our hearts, seeking Him in prayer, and walking in His anointing. Our relationship with Him and one another is where we will either fail or succeed.

✤ It appears the two essential factors in any true revival are God's sovereign dispensation of mercy, grace, and love, and the prayers of those who intercede for revival. Lord, help us to not fail in the great responsibility we have to pray!

✤ Finally, these are days of transition. Church can no longer be "business as usual." Change is coming! The future will be unlike the past; and we must prepare for it.

Days of Decision

Many Christians are simply waiting for the Lord to come and rapture them out of the calamities they see coming upon the earth. This is a very selfish mind-set which misses entirely what is in the Lord's heart. He is coming for a bride who has prepared and given herself to His purpose for these days. The very darkness and difficulties from which men seek to escape are events intended by God to separate out the tares from His kingdom, and prepare the Church to gather in the greatest harvest of souls in the history of Christendom. The river of God's Spirit will sweep over every nation on earth, including the nation of Israel. Multitudes will turn to the Lord as His love, mercy, and compassion are revealed. The gospel of the kingdom will be preached as a witness to all nations before He returns. No one will remain neutral; everyone will have to decide for or against Him.

It is not a time to fly away and escape, but a time to overcome. It is a day to do battle for the souls of men against the world forces of darkness and spiritual authorities in heavenly places.

It is a time of transition. We are entering a new era in the history of the Church, one which is intricately woven into God's purpose for this age. All is on schedule! When the Lord initiated His redemptive plan for mankind, He foreknew all things, and where we are today is exactly where He knew we would be. Nothing has occurred that was not foreknown. At no time has the Lord ever reacted to unexpected circumstances. All is in His hands! We who are alive in Christ today were also foreknown; thus, it is not by accident we have been born for His purpose now, and not in some previous generation. We have been brought to the kingdom for just such a time as this! We dare not simply wait for the climax of this great conflict to come without preparing ourselves for it.

In Review

1. A final great revelation of God's grace and mercy to a lost world will take place, a revival that will be attested to with many supernatural signs and wonders. Unity, love, and compassion in believers will reflect God's

glory on the Church. This will be accompanied by a climax of darkness and deception in the world.

2. The Church, in her present state, is not ready for the task ahead. For that reason, the Lord is sovereignly arising to renew, prepare, and equip His people. The work ahead can only be accomplished by the Holy Spirit. Traditional methods without His anointing would surely fail. A deep preparatory work must be done in hearts through prayer and fasting.

3. The forces that God is mobilizing are not just His armies. His resources include the elements and ecological factors of the world. Earthquakes, famines, hurricanes, droughts, volcanoes, floods, scarcity of commodities, etc., are tools He will use to call men and nations to repentance. These winds of adversity, including persecution, are not to be seen by the church as enemies but as allies (see Rom. 8:17-18,28-29). Such things are not sent to destroy us, but to deepen our roots in Him. They serve to prepare us for His glory.

4. Reality of the love our Father has for us must be developed in our hearts. He is moving in renewal power, doing heart surgery to remove idols that have taken over His rightful place in ours lives. He is calling for the Church to spend more time in His presence. Our success in the days ahead will largely depend on the love relationship we have with our Lord.

5. There will be unity in the body of Christ; this is a critical issue that is essential for the harvest. For too long Christians have tried to unite on the basis of doctrine. The trouble is that once we get our doctrine all defined and well supported by Scripture, we are then divided from others who have defined things differently. Some compromise and sacrifice truth on the altar of ecumenism. Others become so convinced they are correct that

they declare themselves to be the one "true church." The Lord is grieved over the sin of division in His body. The one and only basis He has provided for unity is His glory, His character, His nature.

And the glory which Thou has given Me I have given to them; that they may be one, just as We are one; I in them, and Thou in Me, that they may be perfected in unity...(John 17:22-23).

Only the love of God can draw us to Him and to one another; only God's love enables us to walk in forgiveness and unity.

A new commandment I give to you, that you love one another, even as I have loved you, that you also love one another. By this all men will know that you are My disciples, if you have love for one another (John 13:34-35).

Let us now consider the scope and characteristics of the harvest that lies ahead.

Chapter 2

The Great Harvest

The Feast of Tabernacles

Harvest...that wonderful season when farmers gather in the fruits of their labor.

It has always been harvest time for the Church. The world is a field that has been white for harvest in every generation. The great commission to gather in that harvest has never been completed.

The fields of the world have been experiencing harvest for 2,000 years. However, there will be an ultimate glorious harvest that closes this age of grace.[5] This particular harvest will be a fulfillment of the Feast of Tabernacles (or Feast of Ingathering).

Religious life in Israel during the Old Testament was largely centered around three major feasts, or appointments, each of which pertained to phases of the yearly harvest of their land. These feasts were shadows (or types) of future spiritual harvests that would fulfill them. The first was the Feast of Passover, which was fulfilled in the death and resurrection of Jesus. He was the first fruits of God's spiritual harvest (see 1 Cor. 5:7). The second was the Feast of Pentecost, which was fulfilled by the first outpouring of the Holy Spirit (see Acts 2:1-21). The spiritual harvest of this second feast are all the souls who have been saved since then through the convicting power of the Spirit.

God will conclude the season of harvest with a great ingathering of souls from all nations to fulfill the Feast of Tabernacles. The Lord will then return to close this age of grace by resurrecting and gathering to Himself all who belong to Him (see Rev. 14:14-16). I realize that for years many sincere believers have predicted the immediacy of the Lord's return; time has proven all of them wrong. I do not know when He will return, but as this millennium draws to a close there are many signs pointing to a great ingathering of souls. This could be the final great harvest that will bring His return, which is the burden of my heart.

I believe the greatest release of divine power in the history of the Church lies just ahead, as the gospel of the kingdom is proclaimed and demonstrated to all nations. There is no redemptive power greater than the love of God. When the gospel is proclaimed with mercy, love, and compassion, being confirmed by attesting signs and wonders, multitudes from every nation will come to the Lord![6]

> *And this gospel of the kingdom shall be preached in the whole world for a witness to **all the nations**, and then the end shall come* (Matthew 24:14).

A Harvest That Is Different

The final ingathering that lies ahead for the Church will be quite different from the harvests of all previous revivals. Because of the eternal consequences from what will take place, it is imperative that we understand why this harvest is different, and what makes it so uniquely important. The parable of the tares provides valuable insight.

> *Allow both* (tares and good grain) *to grow together **until the harvest;** and in the time of harvest I will say to the reapers, **"First gather up the tares** and bind them in bundles to burn them up..." **the field is the world**... **the tares are the sons of the evil one...the harvest is the end of the age**....The Son of Man will send His angels, and they will **gather out of His kingdom all stumbling blocks and those who commit lawlessness**. Then the righteous will shine forth as the sun in the kingdom of their Father* (Matthew 13:30,38-39,41,43).

Two distinctions of this harvest are that it is the end of the age, and that, before it is completed, all tares will be gathered out of His kingdom. However, the following are other ways in which this harvest will be different:

❖ The condition of the field

❖ The condition of the grain that is harvested

❖ The season of harvest

❖ The magnitude of the harvest

❖ The sovereignty of God; His role in the harvest

Let us examine each of these differences so as to better prepare ourselves to be profitable laborers.

Condition of the Field

...and the field is the world...(Matthew 13:38).

The harvest field is the entire world, not just a few nations. Individuals and nations are subjected to evil influences from forces on earth, and by spiritual forces of wickedness located in the heavens. The Church is restrained by these rulers and authorities in the heavens, which are specific evil personalities placed by satan over cities, regions, and nations. Through these fallen angels and demons on earth, satan attacks us in many ways; one of his greatest strategies is turning believers against one another to bring disunity in the Church epitomized by the words that God uses to describe satan: "the accuser of our brethren" (see Rev. 12:10).

As this age draws to a close, knowing that his time is short, satan will initiate new heights of lawlessness in both conduct and deception upon the earth (see Mt. 24:4-24; 1 Tim. 4:1). The prophet Isaiah speaks of these days as follows:

> *For behold, darkness will cover the earth and deep darkness the peoples...*(Isaiah 60:2).

Over the years, satan has raised up a militant force of evil against the Church and Israel in Islam, which after Christianity is the fastest growing religion in the world today. A primary doctrine in the Islamic holy books, the Koran and the Hadith (a codified collection of Mohammad's acts and sayings), is the "Jihad." This is a call to all Muslims to wage violent, holy war on "all unbelievers" until Islam reigns as Allah's religion everywhere. As a result, there is opposition and great persecution in nations where Islam is the state religion. Islam is growing in America where it is marked by an aberrant group: The Nation of Islam.

Satan is committed to destroying family life through abortion, homosexuality, and divorce. He knows that the family is God's building block for the Church.

He has targeted the youth for destruction, just as he attempted to thwart the purpose of God in the days of Moses and Jesus by destroying multitudes of children. His assault on the unsaved youth today is devastating, widespread, and growing at an alarming rate. Satan's tools of deception include music (i.e., metallic hard rock and subliminal recorded messages), drugs, the occult, fantasy role playing, pornography, spirit of rebellion against authority, witchcraft and even satanism.

The real issue with satan is spiritual. He has a strategy of deception by which he seeks to be worshipped as god of the world. This can only take place through massive deception designed to touch every sphere of society, including commerce, education, the media, politics, religion, medicine, etc. This is precisely what the "New Age Movement" is all about! Much of the activity of this movement does not appear to be evil and is attractive to those in the world. For example, the currently popular theme of "self" in the secular world (i.e., self-love, self-esteem, self-actualization, etc.), which places "self" instead of God on the throne in individual's lives, is a major doorway into the New Age Movement.

It promises a counterfeit millennium, the astrological "New Age of Aquarius" which is to be an age of enlightenment without the God of the Bible, where man is enthroned. The concepts of God, the world, man, and salvation are taken from classic Hinduism. It is pantheistic in that God and nature are one. There is one ultimate kind of matter for all things. If all is one, then there can be no sin, death, or guilt of sin. Therefore, the substitutionary death of Christ is meaningless. Hinduism agrees that Jesus is God, but no more than we can be. He simply achieved "Christ consciousness," something we can all attain to. The pantheistic God is impersonal, neither speaking nor acting. Space and time are considered illusions. Thus, there is no concept of divine revelation as in Christianity. Rather, spiritual knowledge is available to anyone who, by an "altered state of consciousness," is able to perceive it. This is where demonic deception comes into play. The mental ability to penetrate the illusion of space and time, and thereby achieve this new state of consciousness, comes from mystical occult experiences. For example, using the guidance of mediums, messages are received from spirit beings who falsely identify themselves as "extra-terrestrials from other galaxies," or as persons who have lived on earth at some time in the past. However, they are demons whose objective is to deceive and entrap the listener.

> *But evil men and imposters will proceed from bad to worse, deceiving and being deceived* (2 Timothy 3:13).

In addition to deceiving spirits of the New Age Movement, our day is marked by the overt sins of lawlessness, genocide, terrorism, abortion, drug use, and organized crime. Witchcraft influences many of the decisions made in our social institutions, including even some churches.

To summarize, the following words from pertinent Scriptures describe unsaved inhabitants on earth in the last days: deceivers and deceived, lovers of self, disobedient to parents, lovers of money, boastful, arrogant, revilers, brutal, ungrateful, grumblers, unloving, irreconcilable, haters of good, treacherous, conceited, lovers of pleasures, devoid of the Spirit, worldly minded, mockers, and lawless ones.

In reality, these words describe the field from which the harvest is to be reaped. It becomes immediately apparent that the world today, because of the deep darkness, will be the *most difficult field in history for the Church to reap from.*

Condition of the Grain

In another parable, Jesus describes the condition of many who will be saved in the final harvest.

> *...go out at once into the streets and lanes of the city and bring in here the **poor** and **crippled** and **blind** and **lame**...Go out into the highways and along the hedges, and compel them to come in, that my house may be filled* (Luke 14:21,23).

Statistics from The Mission Handbook[7] paint a vivid picture of the world's harvest field. For example:

❖ By the year 2025, over one quarter of the world's population will be poor and living in squatter settlements. There are today 115 million children between the ages of 6 and 11 who attend no school of any kind.

❖ One person in five lives in poverty so absolute that their survival is at stake daily, and two persons in five are malnourished. In 1990 there were 800 million illiterate adults.

❖ In 1992 there were 25 million children living and sleeping on city streets; 32 million people, many of whom were children, lived in bonded or involuntary servitude. The figures will be higher today.

❖ One third of the world's population is under the age of 15, and 85% of these children live in countries which have high birth rates, and where deprivation and disease, such as AIDS, are widespread. For example, the world's population doubles in approximately 100 years, but it doubles in 17 to 20 years in Kenya, Zambia, Tanzania, Rwanda, and Uganda.

33

✤ At the beginning of 1996 there were 9.6 million persons in Africa who had been forced to flee their homes. As a result of genocide in Rwanda during 1994, when an estimated half million Tutsi were killed by the Hutu tribe, approximately 1.7 million Hutu have fled into Zaire and Tanzania fearing revenge. The end of 1996 sees a potential disaster of disease and poverty among these thousands of displaced refugees.

Through mercy and compassion the Lord will reach out and bring into His kingdom many of the dysfunctional souls that society has discarded. This will include the poor, especially children, of all nations (see Isaiah 58:6-11). He will build His house with broken boards, bent nails, and warped shingles. That which man has thrown away will become precious material in the Lord's hands. We can expect many to come to Christ from the sin-ridden streets of our cities.

This final harvest will be gathered from every region on earth—from the nation of Israel, as well as Islamic countries, Japan, China, and other cultures which today are closed and resistant to the gospel.

We begin to recognize that the grain will not only be more difficult to reap, it will also require greater amounts of godly nurturing and care. Traditional methods alone simply will not suffice. The Lord's heart of mercy, compassion, and love will be needed, so that the Church becomes a spiritual hospital. Without His divine resources much of the grain would be lost.

Thus, we conclude that both the harvest and the discipling of converts from the harvest will be *more challenging than ever before* in Church history!

The Season of Harvest

Following the Reformation, there were long seasons between sowing and reaping in world evangelism. Travel and communication technologies, including literature publication, were in their infancy. Much time was required by missionaries to travel to their foreign field, learn the native language, translate Scripture into that language, and teach the people to read before there were many converts.

There has been a reduction in this time over the centuries as communication, education, and transportation facilities have improved. One significant factor has been the advent of radio as a viable media for preaching the gospel. At the turn of this century, baptism in the Holy Spirit and spiritual gifts were restored to the Church, which empowered and confirmed the gospel message. All of these factors have helped to reduce the time between sowing the word of God and reaping souls for Christ.

At the end of this century, because of technological advances such as television, satellites, video and audio media, there will be a further shortening of the season between sowing and reaping. The Internet will be like a worldwide bookstore where spiritual resources in the form of printed matter, graphics, or even live presentations can be accessed independent of national boundaries. Ministry centers can make renewal and training literature available from web sites to an immense audience with essentially no communication delay. The promise of God points to this trend.

> *Behold, days are coming, declares the Lord, when the plowman will overtake the reaper and the treader of grapes him who sows seeds...*(Amos 9:13).

We are coming to a time when, by the power of God and the use of communication technologies, a great harvest of souls will occur in diverse world-wide localities even as the word of God is being proclaimed.

In other words, not only will the field and the grain be most difficult, but there will essentially be *no season between sowing and reaping*. Talk about a difficult harvest!

Magnitude of the Harvest

Because our human tendency is to calibrate things by what has happened in the past, it is very difficult for us to grasp the dimensions of what lies ahead. There is no pattern for the future; no revival or harvest from the past can compare to the ingathering that will close this age.

Unfortunately, the faith of many believers, especially in America, has been weakened by a theology that projects failure for the end-time Church—where she barely escapes destruction through the rapture, instead of becoming a victorious, overcoming Church that impacts every nation on earth.

God has promised to pour out His Spirit on all mankind (see Joel 2:28-32). This double portion of the Holy Spirit is likened in Scripture to the early (fall) and latter (spring) rains which brought the crops in Israel to a maturity for harvest.

> *And the threshing floors will be full of grain, and the vats will overflow with the new wine and oil* (Joel 2:24).

The harvest will be so great that its abundance will make up for what was not gathered in previous harvests because of satan's demonic attacks and loss of truth by the Church in those years.

*Then I will **make up to you for the years** that the swarming locust has eaten, the creeping locust, the stripping locust, and the gnawing locust...* (Joel 2:25).

The magnitude of the earth's population today, compared to previous centuries, provides support of this wonderful promise. The harvest from the last decades of the church age will dwarf that gathered over the centuries.

In the January 1997 newsletter of *Intercessors for America,* John D. Beckett states: *"...seventy percent of all evangelism that has ever occurred throughout history has occurred in this century. Seventy percent of that evangelism has occurred since World War II, and seventy percent of that evangelism has occurred in the last 36 months."*

The prophet Isaiah describes nations and kings of the earth being drawn to the glory of God resting upon the Church.

*Arise, shine; for your light has come, and the glory of the Lord has risen upon you...But the Lord will rise upon you. **And His glory will appear upon you. And nations will come to your light, and kings to the brightness of your rising*** (Isaiah 60:1-3).

Verses six and seven, in this chapter of Isaiah, identify five regions of Islamic people who will be represented in this company of the redeemed. As fullness of the Gentiles comes to pass, Israel as a nation will also turn to the Lord (see Rom. 11:25). A great ingathering of Semitic peoples!

I believe the greatest release of divine power in the history of the Church lies ahead, as the gospel of the kingdom is proclaimed and demonstrated to all nations. There is no redemptive power greater than the love of God. When the gospel is proclaimed with mercy, love, and compassion, being confirmed by attesting signs and wonders, nations will come to the Lord! Their leaders will not only hear about Jesus, but they will see His gospel demonstrated in love and power. What they had never heard or known, they will see and understand.

> *Thus He will sprinkle many nations, kings will shut their mouths on account of Him; for what had not been told them they will see, and what they had not heard they will understand* (Isaiah 55:12).

> *For thus says the Lord of Hosts, "Once more in a little while I am going to shake the heavens and the earth, the sea also and the dry land. And I will shake all the nations; and they will come with the **wealth** of all nations; and I will fill this house with glory; says the Lord of hosts"* (Haggai 2:6-7).

The Hebrew word used in this verse for "wealth" is *Chemdah.* This word does not refer to wealth in terms of gold, silver, or jewels; nor does it refer to wealth of a nation's military might. There are other Hebrew words for these two expressions of wealth. *Chemdah*, which can also be translated as "desire," refers to what is most precious in God's eyes: the *people* of a nation! Nations and their leaders will come to Him when His glory rises on the Church.

The Lord describes this harvest in another parable, one which concerns the hiring of laborers at different hours of the day to work in a vineyard. These hours of labor over the day represent the total years of harvest in the Church age. The laborers who were hired last, at the eleventh hour, were honored above the other laborers by being paid first at the close of the day—presumably because of the *greater abundance of fruit* they gathered in (see Mt. 20:1-16). Eleventh hour laborers clearly point to those who work in the harvest fields as this age comes to a close. It is possible they will gather in more than all the other laborers combined. It is in this sense that the last shall be first.

All people, in all nations, will be brought to a place of decision as the gospel of the kingdom is proclaimed.

> *Multitudes, multitudes in the valley of decision! For the day of the Lord is near in the valley of decision* (Joel 3:14).

It will be a glorious harvest. The Feast of Tabernacles will close this age as the ultimate and greatest harvest of all time!

The conditions of the field and grain, the magnitude of the harvest, leads us to a fifth difference, one which should be obvious.

The Sovereignty of God

When we consider the first four areas of difference that characterize the final harvest, it becomes apparent that it is an *utterly impossible task* for the Church of today to accomplish. Only the sovereignty of God can bring it to pass; and this will be another difference of the harvest. His hand will be more evident in all that takes place.

> *The Lord has established His throne in the heavens; and His sovereignty rules over all* (Psalm 103:19).

God foreknows all things, and what He has purposed to do will take place; nothing can stop it! Everything taking place in the earth does so within the context of God's permissive or directive will. Consider the following examples of His sovereignty:

❖ Satan can only go as far in his attacks on us as God permits.

❖ It is God who raises up and brings down nations and leaders (see Ps. 47:8). The nation of Israel is a good example.

And He made from one, every nation of mankind to live on all the face of the earth, having determined their appointed times and the boundaries of their habitation (Acts 17:26).

❖ Many are called, but God sovereignly chooses some individuals for His purpose. Abraham, Joseph, and Paul are examples. Reports, such as the story of Father Hilberto Gomez in Mexico, point to contemporary examples.

❖ Church history reveals that God has sovereignly moved many times during periods of backsliding to revive His inheritance. The "Great Awakening" is one such example. Revivals are fruits of His sovereignty, not because He sends good things to us, but because He comes Himself.

And that is what the Lord is beginning to do today. He is sovereignly bringing His "fire" into the Church! He is preparing His body to bring in the harvest; and our need is very great! The darkness that will cover the earth is evident today, but where is the glory?

Disunity is pervasive in the Church. While there are many good programs and much zeal to evangelize, there is not the love, mercy, and compassion necessary to effectively bring in the poor, crippled, blind, and lame from our streets; nor is the power of God present as it should be to demonstrate the gospel of the kingdom.

We can't imagine the great work that the Lord will do through a united Church that with purity of heart is committed to worship and intercession for lost souls—a Church crowned with the glory of God!

One's flesh cannot help but respond when God touches our innermost being so deeply. Rational minds may be offended; but He is after our hearts, which is where renewal takes place.

The transition of renewal will not be without pain. Psychological and demonic components can be expected to surface, as well as attention-seeking behavior. Good leadership will handle such things so that they do not detract from the purpose of God. As the Lord moves in renewal power, some in the church may oppose what is taking place. However, they will not be able to withstand the sovereignty of God.

The glory will appear on the Church as hearts are purified and His people come into greater intimacy with Him. There can be no glory on the Church apart from repentance, humility, and unity. There is no place for pride or self sufficiency. As Lord of the harvest, He alone will receive all the glory, for He alone can bring it to pass.

As sin increases in the world, there will also be an increase in persecution, suffering, and even martyrdom for some believers. However, God will sovereignly increase His grace as He reaches out to all mankind in a final great demonstration of love and mercy before the day of His wrath and judgment comes. This grace, which reveals the love and compassion of Jesus, is where our hope is to be focused.

Therefore, gird up your minds for action, keep sober in spirit, fix your hope completely on the grace to be brought to you at the revelation of Jesus Christ (1 Peter 1:13).

A significant aspect of God's renewal today is His sovereign work in the hearts of children, preparing them for the days ahead. Possibly because He knows this: satan is seeking to destroy the youth of today. It is quite possible that the eleventh hour laborers will come from today's children and youth. This highlights the great responsibility that parents and church leaders have in training the children, a ministry that was foretold by the prophet Malachi (see Mal. 4:5-6).

There is great peace and comfort in knowing that all things are in His sovereign hands; the future is certain. It is a time to rejoice!

The last unique distinction of the harvest that we will consider concerns the tares.

The Tares

The final harvest is the time when tares will be gathered out from among the good grain. This is a significant difference from all previous revivals. Tares look like true grain. However, at harvest time grain will bend low with the weight of ripe kernels, whereas tares stand erect having no fruit. Throughout Church history, tares have always existed among the grain. A vital part of this harvest will be the removal of all tares. These individuals are referred to by Jesus as stumbling blocks or those who commit lawlessness (see Mt. 13:30,39-43).

This purging work of the Holy Spirit will prepare the bride for her Lord's return; once the tares are gone, the saints will shine forth as the sun in the kingdom of their Father. Hence, the final harvest will not only be a day of ingathering, but also a day of separation and purification.

Just as many will be drawn to the Lord because of God's glory upon the Church, others will fear the glory and run from the light because their deeds are evil. Because these individuals will not receive the truth so as to be saved, they shall be deceived and drawn away by the mystery of lawlessness that even today is at work in the world.

This will take place through a climax in lawlessness brought about by a visible unveiling of the man of lawlessness, the son of destruction, to the world (see 2 Thess. 2:3). He will be an incarnation of evil who works great, lying signs and wonders of deception. God will allow this revelation of evil to become a deluding influence upon those who refuse to come to Him, so that they might believe what is false.

> *And for this reason God will send upon them a deluding influence so that they might believe what is false, in order that they all may be judged who did not believe the truth, but took pleasure in wickedness* (2 Thessalonians 2:11-12).

Thus, in a time of great shaking and spiritual warfare, tares will be gathered out of God's kingdom. The glory of the Lord will then rest in new measure upon His people. The bride will be prepared for her Lord's return.

The Open Heavens

The unique and significant event that brings about this climax of good and evil is satan and his angels being thrown down to the earth from their place in the heavens. At this time, he will know that he has but a short time left (see Rev. 12:12).

A great hindrance to the Church is the oppressive, restraining influence of evil by principalities and powers in heavenly places. Satan is prince of the power of the air (see Eph. 2:2). Spirits of condemnation, deception, despair, depression, hopelessness, etc., in concert with satan's accusations, are constantly opposing the saints.

As a consequence, God will sovereignly arise to shake all things, not only on earth but in the heavens as well (see Heb. 12:25-29). Powers of the heavens will be shaken (see Mt. 24:29). It will be a time of intense persecution for believers, with martyrdom becoming a doorway to glory for some (see Rev. 12:11; Mt. 24:9-13,21-24). Overcomers will arise (see Rev. 2:26-27; 3:12,21; 2 Tim. 2:11-12). Unity and power will mark the body of Christ. The ministry of angels will be commonplace.

It will be a time of great spiritual warfare through intercession, worship, and the gospel of the kingdom. In the heavens, warfare will be waged by the army of angels led by Michael, whom God releases to do battle with satan and his angels (see Dan. 12:1; Rev. 12:7).

The result of this cosmic warfare will see satan and his angels cast down onto the earth (see Rev. 12:8-9). This climactic event has two major consequences:

❖ Heaven will be open above the Church. There will no longer exist the hindering influence of satan, the accuser of our brethren, in the heavens. As a result, great power and authority will rest upon the Church, resulting in signs and wonders never seen before on earth. It will be a time of great supernatural miracles (see Jn. 14:12).

> *...now the salvation, and the power, and the kingdom of our God and the authority of His Christ have come, **for the accuser of our brethren has been thrown down**, who accuses them before our God day and night* (Revelation 12:10).

❖ Being cast into the earth, satan will impart all his power and authority into the man of sin. This son of destruction will become visibly present in the world; through great lying signs and wonders, he will deceive all who dwell on the earth whose names are not written in the Lamb's book of life (see Rev. 13:8).

Paul's second epistle to Thessalonica presents a scenario of this man of sin's appearance. Paul's words reveal how the Lord uses the deception of satan's false signs and wonders to gather out the tares. The pertinent Scripture is taken from the *Concordant Literal New Testament* because of a more accurate translation of the Greek words, *Ginomai* meaning "to be" or "to become," and *Mesos* meaning "midst" (see Appendix).

> *And now you are aware what (or who) is detaining (or restraining) for him to be unveiled in his own era. For the secret of lawlessness is already operating. Only when the present detainer may be **coming to be** out of the **midst*** (2 Thessalonians 2:6,7).

> *And **then that lawless one will be revealed** whom the Lord will slay with the breath of His mouth and bring to an end by the appearance of His coming* (2 Thessalonians 2:8).

Satan is and will continue to be a restraining influence in the heavens against the Church until the day that he and his angels are cast down onto the earth. At that time, in order to be worshipped as god, he will invest his power and authority in a man through whom the fullness of his lawlessness

45

becomes suddenly visible to the world. Thus the man of lawlessness will come to be (or appears) out of the midst of mankind. He will deceive unbelievers by lying signs and wonders, which God allows to take place, in order to gather together all who would not be saved. After that takes place there will no longer be any tares among the good grain, and the righteous will shine as the sun in the kingdom of their Father (see Mt. 13:24-43)!

Culmination of the harvest will then take place when the Lord Jesus returns to gather His Church to Himself; at that time He will destroy the lawless one by the brightness of His coming. The following are Scriptures that describe this glorious harvest finale: Daniel 7:13-27; Matthew 24:27-31; 1 Corinthians 15:49-51; 2 Thessalonians 4:13-18; Revelations 14:14-16.

Looking Ahead

We cannot anticipate the future based on what has happened in the past. There is no pattern in Church history that will foretell what lies ahead. Like Noah, we must prepare for unheard of times that we have never before experienced.

> *Do not call to mind the former things or ponder things of the past. Behold, I will do something new, now it will spring forth; will you not be aware of it...* (Isaiah 43:18-19).

The Church today is not in a position spiritually for the task ahead, and God is sovereignly arising to prepare her. A deep work is being done in hearts. We need a passion for God, one that will intercede in love, mercy, and compassion for the lost, while recognizing that it will not be by our might or power, but by His Spirit, that the harvest will be brought in.

Our Father is revealing how much He loves us just as we are! As we respond to His overtures of love, He changes us, for we must have His heart to be successful in the harvest field. And we must increase our love for one another, for unity is absolutely vital!

We have to prepare for great shaking. Much that has been built in the Church will be found wanting. Humility is truly essential in our lives for Jesus to change us and to become Lord and Head of His body.

Lord, light the fire in our hearts; reveal Your glory in the face of Your Son. Prepare us as the reapers for the harvest ahead.

Chapter 3

Preparing the Reapers

The Place to Start

We stand on the threshold of a mighty work by God. One that concerns all nations and all peoples. Through prophets, He has been calling the Church to prepare for harvest.

How does one prepare? The task appears so monumental that it is hard to comprehend, let alone to accomplish. However, the future is not to be feared. All is in His hands!

The first step in preparing oneself is to recognize the sovereignty of God in our personal life. Each believer has an important part to play in the purpose of God for his generation. The place of service God has prepared for us was in His heart when He formed us in our mother's womb. We are really no different than Jeremiah or David in this respect (see Jer. 1:5; Ps. 139:13-16). Knowing the environments of our childhood and adult lives, our parents, the specific problems and circumstances we would face, our education, employment, spouse, geographic location, etc., the Lord has allotted grace and placed certain qualities within us to perform the service He would later call and anoint us for. We are His handiwork created in Christ Jesus for works of service that He has already prepared for us to walk in. And these works are specific for the day in which we live. We have been brought to the kingdom for just this time!

As individuals, each of us possess diverse latent abilities and personalities that make us special to Him. We have been created to fill a unique place of service in the body of Christ. We are not to see our place of service as insignificant; nor are we to see our problems, circumstances, or call as too great for us!

Our personal qualities and abilities have no value in the kingdom until we are saved and have laid down all that we are and own at the foot of the cross. The goal in doing so is to establish His Lordship; only when we are convinced of our weakness can He be strong in us. Once this is done, the next step is to prepare for the spiritual realm. How do we proceed?

There is but one place where this preparation can take place, and that is in His presence. It is not the teaching we hear or the trials and circumstances we go through that, by themselves, effect change within us. Only to the extent that such things draw us into His presence for more grace, mercy, and understanding will we be prepared. At His feet we will learn to hear His heart and distinguish His ways.

It is He Himself, not our ministry, our goals, or our call that must become the desire of our hearts. It is Jesus alone, nothing else!

Prepared Hearts

The most important issue in preparation is our hearts. We simply do not appreciate how horrible sin is in God's eyes. In our walk with Him, He sees us just as we are in our hearts (see Prov. 27:19). Unfortunately, apart from the Holy Spirit, we are unable to see or judge our heart as He does, much less the hearts of others.

The heart is more deceitful than all else and is desperately sick; who can understand it? (Jeremiah 17:9)

To write on this subject one must begin by first examining his own heart, and I confess that my heart is not yet prepared for what lies ahead. I don't weep over the state of lost souls, and I am more likely to feel sorry for dysfunctional persons than to be moved with compassion and intercede for them. I am a good example of why the Church needs revival! My responsibility is clear:

Watch over your heart with all diligence, *for from it flows the springs of life* (Proverbs 4:23).

Too many believers walk somewhere between the following two verses:

Blessed are the pure in heart, for they shall see God (Matthew 5:8).

Everyone who is proud in heart is an abomination to the Lord (Proverbs 16:50.

Pride is the father of all sin. It destroys our relationship with the Lord and with one another. Pride leads to unforgiveness and opens one up to deception. Pride in leaders brings control and manipulation that prevents Jesus from functionally being head of His Church. The humility of repentance is where heart preparation begins.

God's Call for Humility

If the body of Christ can be likened to a great motor, love would be the fuel that drives the motor, and humility would be the oil of relationship between moving parts.

We are saved by grace, we stand by grace, we grow in grace, we minister by grace, and grace is God's bridge of love to the lost. Given these truths, what is the bottom line? Why is humility so important?

> *...All of you, clothe yourselves with humility toward one another, for God is opposed to the proud, but gives grace to the humble* (1 Peter 5:5).

It is very simple; without humility there will be no grace!

The problems, relationships, and ministries of a local church provide the environment God has ordained to equip believers for service. The importance of humility in the discipling process is seen in the following Scriptures:

> *Do nothing from selfishness or empty conceit,* **but with humility of mind** *let each of you regard one another as more important than himself* (Philippians 2:3).

> *And so, as those who have been chosen of God, holy and beloved, put on a heart of compassion, kindness,* **humility,** *gentleness and patience; bearing with one another, and forgiving each other, whoever has a complaint against anyone; just as the Lord forgave you, so also should you* (Colossians 3:12-13).

There is *no* place for pride in the house of God.

In the coming revival that will sweep the earth, there will be ever greater demonstrations of the love, power, and authority of Christ through the Church. It will be important for ministers to clothe their lives and ministries with humility. To this end, fasting and prayer are vital. The church will be tested and purified as God moves in mighty revival power. There will be temptations to follow after and honor those whom the Lord anoints in ministries of supernatural signs and wonders. This must not happen; no church or man shall be exalted. Pride can destroy those who turn aside to seek personal glory. It is important to heed the prophetic promises and warnings that are coming forth in the renewal.

The Lord is visiting His people with the glory of revival power to prepare them for the darkness. For with the glory will come darkness. Seducing spirits and false prophets will abound, and many who are not prepared in their hearts will fall away (see 1 Tim. 4:1-3; 2 Tim. 3:1-13; Mt. 24:4-11). Our eyes must be kept on the Lord Jesus Christ, and our confidence in the message of His cross.

God is sovereignly touching the hearts of men, women, and children, revealing how very much He loves us. Much of what was theory before, concerning our relationship with Him, is now becoming very real. The first fruit in renewal concerns our relationship with Him. He is calling us to humble ourselves as little children and draw near to Him. As we respond, He will deal with idols in our lives such as pride, personal goals, worldly pleasures, religious agendas, hidden sins, etc. These idols have replaced Him in our hearts, and He will not tolerate them for they prevent the intimacy that He seeks with us.

As He moves in renewal power, each believer will face the challenge of humility. For example:

❖ It requires humility to lay down "business-as-usual" religious programs, and give the Lord back His Church.

53

❖ It requires humility for a father to ask forgiveness from his family for past failures.

❖ It requires humility for married couples to seek forgiveness from one another for mistakes that have injured their relationship.

❖ It requires humility to forgive those who have offended or hurt us in the past.

❖ It requires humility to be accountable to those who have oversight in our lives.

❖ It requires humility for leaders to give up their control and allow Jesus to functionally be head of His Church.

❖ It requires humility to adopt a more sacrificial life-style in order to minister to the poor.

❖ The Holy Spirit is not pre-programmed and it requires humility to accept how He moves when it is outside our religious comfort zone.

❖ It requires humility to lay down traditional worship and allow the Holy Spirit to lead us as priests into the presence of God. Anointed worship breaks the oppression of darkness and brings prophetic direction to the Church.

❖ It requires humility to repent of divisiveness and to become open and honest with others, so that there is reality in our relationships.

❖ It requires humility to keep our hands off the glory. We all face the following test:

The crucible is for silver and the furnace for gold, but a man is tested by the praise accorded him (Proverbs 27:21).

As the Lord prepares hearts, His word calls out to us:

Take My yoke upon you, and learn from Me, for I am **gentle** *and* **humble in heart**; *and you will find rest for your souls* (Matthew 11:29).

...But to this one I will look, to him who is **humble** *and* **contrite of spirit**, *and who trembles at My word* (Isaiah 66:2).

Streams in the Desert

In 1989, a conference was held at Indianapolis in which many streams of believers came together in an expression of charismatic unity. I had been invited to speak to the Anabaptist group. As I prepared for the conference, the Lord gave me the following prophetic insight on unity.

I found myself in a desert where everything was very dry and parched. Then the Lord opened my eyes, and I saw scattered across the face of the desert, a large number of streams with the water of life flowing in them. The Lord revealed to me that the desert represents the condition of believers who have become dry and barren in their hearts and where the Holy Spirit has ceased to flow among them.

However, the Lord said that, in time, one in such a group will recognize the great need to seek Him in repentance, and to move forward in the purpose of God. When this happens, the Lord extends grace to this person, who by faith, will begin to dig a trench in the sand. As he does so, the Holy Spirit fills the trench and a stream of the water of life begins to flow in it. Each stream then takes on an identity that is related to the grace and vision of the one digging.

Somehow I knew that each stream represented various bodies and denominations of believers who have pressed on to know the Lord after that body had lost the fullness and reality of His life among them. They began to dig streams of renewal and restoration!

As I considered the various streams, I saw that they were often quite different from one another. For example, some were short in length while others were long and one or two were very long indeed; some were narrow and others were quite wide; some were straight and others displayed numerous bends and changes in directions. The latter were those bodies of believers where traditions and dogma had to be circumvented in digging that stream.

However, all streams appeared to be headed in the same direction, generally running in parallel with one another, but never joining together. I then noticed a few steams that had become so shallow they simply ceased to exist. I also noticed that, in some instances, beside these dry stream beds, a fresh stream had broken forth and was flowing on, bearing an identity that appeared to be related to the dry stream.

I decided to walk forward in the direction toward which the streams were flowing. As I went, I saw several new streams that had just emerged in the desert.

Finally, I came to a new stream that was different from the others. It was much deeper, and its direction of flow, while forward, was somewhat transverse to the other streams so that eventually each one would intersect it. I also noticed that, unlike other streams, its identity was not related to an individual; it was called "humility."

I observed that as the many streams eventually flowed into "humility," they became united. The result was a mighty increase in the power and force of the water of life as it flowed forward through the desert.

As I looked to see where this new stream was headed, I saw that it flowed into a great river that was too deep to ford. This was the river of life flowing from the throne of God! As the various streams entered into this river, I realized each one had totally lost all identity. Only the Lord and His name remained!

The One Body of Christ

The world places great value on objects that are rare. One who owned the only remaining original painting by a famous painter would be wealthy.

However, Christians often seem unaware that they are part of a uniquely rare masterpiece put together by the greatest Master of all time, the Lord Jesus Christ. They belong to the *one* and *only* body in Christ, an organism created by the Spirit of God and made up of all true believers in Christ.

*So we, who are many, are **one** body in Christ, and individually members one of another* (Romans 12:5).

That we believers generally do not grasp the great value there is in this one body can be seen by how we point out differences between our group and others more often than we emphasize the communion (or life-union) with Christ that is common among us. For this reason, the uniqueness that the Lord intends in life, structure, service, and vision for His body often becomes blurred by human programs and methodologies. The body of Christ has become a denominated array of human institutions which mask the organism of divine life that makes it unique. The Lord states that we are one body in Him and members one of another. It is these two aspects of life-union that make the body of Christ unique.

Lack of unity between churches is a weakness. However, we are living in a time of Church renewal and restoration. Who can possibly measure the value of His glorious presence in bringing unity to the Church? It is beyond our comprehension; yet unity is coming, and this is where our hope and vision is to be.

Becoming Part of the Body

No one can join the body of Christ; one must be born into it, a supernatural act that only the Spirit of God can perform.

> *For by one Spirit we were all baptized into one body, whether Jews or Greeks, whether slaves or free, and we were all made to drink of one Spirit* (1 Corinthians 12:13).

Through faith and repentance, we are spiritually born into the family of God, the Holy Spirit placing or baptizing us into the body of Christ. We then have a life-union with Christ through His Spirit. This communion, or fellowship in the Spirit, is what constitutes the Church. We need not have the same understanding of Scriptures as do other believers; we need only possess the same divine life. Apart from faith, repentance and confession, a believer can contribute nothing to the miracle of regeneration. Even faith is only possible through the grace of God. No wonder salvation is a gift!

For by grace you have been saved through faith; and that not of yourselves, it is the gift of God; not as a result of works, that no one should boast (Ephesians 2:8-9).

Simple, clear literature on the essentials of salvation is a vital tool for evangelism.

Holy Trinity Brompton in London, England is an Anglican church that has been impacted by the Toronto renewal. Under the leadership of the vicar, Sandy Millar, this church prepared the Alpha Course, an 11-week "easy to understand" introduction to Jesus. It has proven so successful, that at the present rate, roughly 5 million people will have been through the course by the year 2000.

It is important to instruct new converts that salvation involves more than the privilege of one day going to heaven. They have been supernaturally placed into the living organism that God has ordained to accomplish His purpose on the earth. The practical implication of this is to become rooted into a local church. This is the place of preparation and equipping, the place where lives are built together on Christ, the cornerstone.

Equipped With Power

The gospel of the kingdom is more than a logical rationale for righteousness; it is a demonstration of power against evil by the anointing of the Holy Spirit (see Is. 61:1-2; Acts 8:5-8; Rom. 15:18-19). Gifts of the Holy Spirit are not an option; we are commanded to seek and exercise these gifts (see 1 Cor. 12).

The promise of Jesus is still valid today:

But you shall receive power when the Holy Spirit has come upon you; and you shall be My witnesses... (Acts 1:8).

The certainty and clarity of God's call on my life came on the day that I was baptized in the Holy Spirit. I had been saved for several months, but my ministry was birthed in my heart on that wonderful day.

The anointed gospel is our weapon against ignorance, unbelief, and sin in the lives of men, women, and children. The indwelling Holy Spirit is our power to proclaim the gospel and to free captives from demonic spirits such as depression, condemnation, despair, deception, sickness, etc. Deliverance must also deal with the root cause for these bondages, which is often wrong thought or habit patterns that have become fortresses of demonic influence in the mind. God's promise is that He would pour out His Spirit on *all mankind*, that He would anoint men, women, and even children as His witnesses in the last days (see Joel 2:28-29). Children can and will be used in spiritual gifts. It is a great error to think that only men, or adults, can be anointed for ministry in the harvest.

However, power in spiritual warfare is more than having had an experience; it requires a lifestyle based on the indwelling Holy Spirit (see Zech. 4:6). Humility and repentance come before renewal; worship and prayer come before power. Worship and intercession are essential life-style disciplines for spiritual warfare. Worship brings us into His presence where the burden of His heart is revealed. We are then able to intercede accordingly and see the enemy bound.

Let the godly ones exult in glory; let them sing for joy on their beds. Let the high praises of God be in their mouth, and a two-edged sword in their hand, to execute vengeance on the nations, and punishment on the peoples; to bind their kings with chains, and their nobles with fetters of iron; to execute on them the judgment written; this is an honor for all His godly ones. Praise the Lord! (Psalm 149:5-9)

Finally, believers around the world will see greater evidence of God's guidance and power in the days ahead. Prophetic revelations, dreams, visions, powerful demonstrations of spiritual gifts, and ministry of angels will become increasingly common.

Built Upon God's Cornerstone

One cannot impart to others what he does not have himself. How well one is equipped for the harvest fields depends on how well his life is built upon God's cornerstone (see Acts 4:11-12). The quality of life in church plants will also depend on how well they have been built on the same cornerstone, the Lord Jesus Christ (see Eph. 2:19-22).

Behold, I lay in Zion a choice stone, a precious cornerstone, and he who believes in Him shall not be disappointed (1 Peter 2:6).

God Himself has laid this costly cornerstone, one that He has tested and firmly placed for the foundation, and which cannot be moved (see Is. 28:16). The issue all believers face is how to build upon it. (see 1 Cor. 3:10-15). How does one build with gold, silver, and precious stones, and not with wood, hay, and straw? The answer lies in appropriating all that Christ has provided for us as the cornerstone of our faith.

The size of any cornerstone will vary depending upon the dimensions of the building it supports. However, its shape is not arbitrary. A cornerstone supports a maximum load when it is rectangular with uniform thickness, having smooth parallel surfaces on the top and bottom, on the two sides, and on the two ends. A long thin stone would easily break; non-uniform thickness would place all the weight on high parts of the stone. Thus, the key requirement of the cornerstone is to possess correct thickness and have three pairs of smooth parallel surfaces.

It is wonderful to see how the Lord Jesus Christ is the perfect and complete cornerstone for our faith. This is apparent through three pairs of specific provisions of His person and ministry.

I will address these properties in pairs, each pair representing opposite surfaces of a cornerstone which correspond to two provisions of Christ as our cornerstone. Walking in the truths of these provisions is how one builds with gold, silver, and precious stones.

✣ Bottom and top surfaces:
   The bottom surface, which is the supporting level for everything, speaks of the *lordship of Christ*. This directs us to obey and submit to Him in our personal lives. This right belongs to Him, for He has bought us with His blood.

   *That if you confess with your mouth Jesus **as Lord**, and believe in your heart that God raised Him from the dead, you shall be saved* (Romans 10:9).

   The lordship of Christ should not be separated from His role as Savior. If He is our Savior, He is also our Lord! Being our Lord means that His will for us becomes the most important thing in our lives. Submitting to His lordship keeps us from going our own way. Legalism weakens the truth and practice of His lordship.

The top surface speaks of the *headship of Christ*. He has been made head over all things in the Church, which is His body. The significance of Jesus being the head is that all life flows, all anointing, all ministry, all direction, and all unction begin in Him, who is the head, and flows out to the appropriate members in the Church. An organism can have only one head, and these life functions of the Head cannot be delegated to another member. Where lordship points to obedience and submission, headship points to our relationship with Him (see Col. 2:19; Eph. 1:22). However, there can be no headship if there is not lordship. They are interdependent qualities, represented by the two surfaces being parallel. The truth of His headship is weakened by too much emphasis on programs, control, and agendas by leaders. The quality of one's spiritual life and service will stand or fall on the truths of these two surfaces.

❖ The two side surfaces:
One side speaks of the *humanity of Jesus*.

*There is one God and one mediator between God and men, **the man Christ Jesus*** (1 Timothy 2:5).

Jesus referred to Himself as "the son of man" more often than any other way.

Jesus could never have been the cornerstone if He had not been a man. Because satan caused Adam to sin, God ordained that satan be defeated by a man, one who would restore mankind to righteousness and eternal life (see Heb. 2:14-15). It was necessary for that man to keep all of the Law perfectly, which Jesus did. As a result, the righteousness He imputes to us is perfect. It was also necessary for that man to pay the penalty for all sin, past, present, and future, committed by mankind. The Law had to be satisfied in every sense. This Jesus did also, so that any and all sin can be forgiven. He was the last Adam, as God judged the sin of Adam once and for all time. When Jesus went to the cross, He took with Him our human Adamic nature which was nailed with Him to the cross (see Gal. 2:20). The certificate of debt consisting of decrees against us was also nailed to His cross (see Col. 2:14). Thus, once we have been born again, we can be baptized in water where our old carnal nature is cut away, and we arise from the water to walk in victory over sin. We are buried with Him through baptism into death, in order that as Christ was raised from the dead through the glory of the Father, so we too might emerge to walk in newness of life (see Rom. 6:4-6). Too often the truth of water baptism is neglected when discipling believers. All we will ever need to walk in righteousness has been provided for us through the cross of Christ!

*In Him also you were circumcised with a circumcision not made with hands, but in a [spiritual] circumcision [performed by] Christ by stripping off the body of the flesh [the whole corrupt, carnal nature with its passions and lusts]. **[Thus you were circumcised when] you were buried with Him in [your] baptism**...* (Colossians 2:11-12 AMP).

Through the cross satan was totally defeated by the man Christ Jesus, and we have the privilege of walking day by day in His victory.

The surface on the opposite side is related to the humanity of Jesus. It is the priesthood of Jesus; He is *our*

High Priest. He could never have become our High Priest if He had not first been tempted and then overcame temptation as a man. Because He was tempted, He knows our weaknesses and is able to intercede for us (see Heb. 7:25). This involves more than what He experienced in His years of ministry; it includes His life as a child obeying His parents, as a young man helping Joseph, and later as a carpenter, supporting the family. He was tested at every phase of human life.

*Therefore, He had to be made like His brethren in **all things**, that He might become a merciful and faithful High Priest in things pertaining to God, to make propitiation for the sins of the people. For **since He Himself was tempted** in that which He suffered, He is able to come to the aid of those who are tempted* (Hebrews 2:17-18).

It is a priceless privilege to know that we have a great High Priest who not only loves us, but, understanding all that we are going through, is praying for us night and day! He could not be our High Priest if He had not first overcome satan as a man.

These two parallel side surfaces represent interdependent truths that enable us to walk in victory over the world, the flesh, and the devil through the provisions of His cross, and His intercession for us.

❖ The two end surfaces:
One surface speaks of the *divinity of Jesus.* He was Immanuel, God with us. He was begotten by the Holy Spirit, so that the blood in His veins was the blood of God. As the Lamb of God, His blood was efficacious as the perfect sacrifice for sin. The cornerstone *could not be adequate* unless Jesus was God! In addition to His

sacrificial death, a primary role of Jesus was to reveal the Father and make His purpose known to mankind (see Jn. 1:18). His words, deeds, love, compassion, and mercy expressed the Father's heart—something only God could do. Jesus revealed that He and His Father were one, that the Father lived His life in Jesus and was the One who did the works. As we embrace His will, abide in Him and allow Him to live His life in us, we will come into God's purpose for us as His sons (see Eph. 1:3-11). This purpose begins to be realized once we have been baptized with the Holy Spirit. It is a deepening incarnation as we mature and Christ becomes formed in our hearts (see Eph. 3:16-19). He is to be seen in our lives just as the Father was seen in His life (see Rom. 8:14-19; Heb. 2:10).

The Father's heart and purpose to bring forth a family of sons, patterned after the image of Jesus, could never take place apart from coming to earth to reveal and demonstrate His purpose through the life, ministry, and person of His Son.

The opposite end surface speaks of Jesus *being the good Shepherd*. This final surface represents His ministry of shepherding and guiding us into His Father's purpose (see Ps. 23). It is one thing to know God's purpose for our lives; it is quite another to have One guide and lead us into that purpose. The truths of all the other surfaces are brought together in this ministry of Jesus. As our Shepherd, He guides us into all truth, through all opposition and all difficulties into His plan for our lives. We are responsible to hear and obey His voice.

I am the good shepherd; and I know My own, and My own know Me.... And I have other sheep, which are not of this fold; I must bring them also, and they shall hear

My voice; and they shall become one flock with one shepherd (John 10:14,16).

We are to be accountable to those who care for us as His undershepherds. They are responsible to teach us His ways, how to seek Him and to know His voice, without taking His place in our lives.

How securely we are anchored on the cornerstone, how well our life and ministry draws from the living truths of these six surfaces, determines how well we are prepared for the harvest fields and equipped to establish converts in church plants.

The Centrality of Jesus

There is only one true center of emphasis in the body of Christ; that is Christ Himself! It is not dogma, creeds, doctrine, ministry, church government, the gospel, the church, the Bible, the sacraments, or anything else. Only if this emphasis of Christ is restored to the center of Christian faith can the present divisions in the body of Christ be removed and the full witness of Christ in the Church be seen.

The Church, which is His body, is the vehicle that the Lord has chosen to express Himself through. Thus, all that is done or spoken in ministry should always point people to the Lord Jesus Christ. All authority in Heaven and on earth has been given to Him. For this reason, all deeds and proclamations in the Church are to be done in the name of the Lord Jesus Christ (see Col. 3:17).

*For **from** Him and **through** Him and **to** Him are **all** things. To Him be the glory forever* (Romans 11:36).

67

*And He is before **all** things, and **in** Him **all** things hold together...For it was the Father's good pleasure for **all** the fulness to dwell in Him* (Colossians 1:17,19).

Finding Our Place in the Body

We don't decide where we fit in the body of Christ or what our ministry gifts are. These have been determined by the Lord long before we were saved or even born. Our responsibility is to recognize who is in charge of our life and to obey Him. We must seek Him to discover His call on our life (see 2 Tim. 1:9).

But now God has placed the members, each one of them, in the body, just as He desired (1 Corinthians 12:18).

But one and the same Spirit works all these things (i.e., spiritual gifts), distributing to each one individually just as He wills (1 Corinthians 12:11).

Each believer has been prepared in his mother's womb for a unique place of service. Knowing the event profile, the talents, opportunities, strengths, weaknesses, and failures of each child of God, the Lord provides sufficient grace to everyone to fulfill the call on his life. The question is not how visible and grand, or how apparently insignificant one's call might be. The important issue is our commitment to what God has called us to be and to do. We are not to measure ourself, or our success in ministry, by comparison with other believers; each of us stands or falls in the eyes of our Lord. It is vital to recognize the fact that the Lord sees *each* member of His body as equal both in worth and as recipients of His love. The grace we receive will be different, for this relates to our specific call in Christ. We have all been normalized at the cross of Christ; there all men are made equal!

When God called me into the ministry it was with a vision to build "new testament" churches. I am still learning what this means.

One day the Lord revealed to me that correct organizational structure is not the basis for producing His life; it is the other way around; His life produces the structure! To love and be loved, to pray for others and receive their prayers are relational dynamics of the Lord building His body.

My wife and I greatly value the bonds of love that we have had over the years with members of our local church. We are a family, not an organization.

The reality is that we are indeed members of one another and that, together, we form a living expression of the body of Christ.

> *For the body is not one member, but many. If the foot should say, "Because I am not a hand, I am not part of the body," it is not for this reason any less a part of the body...If the whole body were an eye, where would the hearing be? If the whole body were hearing, where would the sense of smell be? ...And the eye cannot say to the hand, "I have no need of you," or again the head to the feet, "I have no need of you"* (1 Corinthians 12:14-17,21).

The heart of revival is how much our heavenly Father loves us. He wants us to rest in His arms of love; He knows all who belong to Him and He loves each one equally. It is a love that changes us, creating a desire for His presence above all else; an ardent "love sickness" for Jesus that reaches out to backsliders and the lost. Revival is a time of rejoicing as prodigals are restored, as forgiveness is extended, and the family of God is completed!

When problems arise, or when one is confronted because of sin in his personal life, the temptation is to leave and find a "better" church. However, this is not the way to maturity. It is important to stay where the Lord has placed us so that He can equip and build us into His body as He pleases. We need to embrace the cross of His discipline for our lives in order to develop strong roots in Him. This is how we grow spiritually. It is a great weakness in the body of Christ when members with personal problems leave one assembly and go to another, being received with no questions asked.

Prepared for Body Ministry

To live, a physical body requires more than all the various organs performing their specific functions in an independent manner. The body lives because the organs work together in harmony. For example, lungs cannot bring oxygen into the blood stream apart from the muscles associated with breathing; blood cannot carry pure oxygen throughout the body apart from the heart and kidneys; and most important of all, there must be directive intelligence from the brain for all organs to function together. It is no different in the body of Christ.

Just as tendons, joints, and sinews are necessary for toes, fingers, arms, and legs to function, so also there must be a synergistic relationship in the Spirit for members of a team to be jointly effective in ministry. An ideal small-group environment for such training, and the bonding of lives together, is in house churches (i.e., cell groups).

> *...holding fast to the head (Christ), from whom the entire body, being supplied and held together by the joints and*

ligaments, grows with a growth which is from God (Colossians 2:19).

Team ministry requires humility, submission, love, and mutual acceptance between members. This is *not* something one learns by simply being taught how to perform, for it is as much related to what we *are* in Christ as to what we *do* for Him.

We also need the ministry and input of brothers and sisters into our lives to encourage, exhort, edify, admonish, and adjust us. We will not make it alone. Body ministry is more than an impersonal transfer of information; it is a sharing of divine life that flows out of the love and acceptance of God.

We have all been created with an innate desire to be loved and accepted. To be rejected can cripple the human spirit. The following are well-known examples of such rejection: children who have been abused by parents; spouses who have been demeaned, abused, or divorced by their mate; individuals who have been shunned because of their race, culture, or disability (physical and mental); and those rejected by society, such as the homeless poor.

At the cross, Christ bore all such rejection and, in particular, our rejection by God because of sin. We have been made acceptable to our heavenly Father through His beloved Son. We have become part of the family of God where all are accepted and loved equally as sons and daughters. The next step is developing the fruit of His acceptance in the body of Christ. Just as Christ has accepted us, we must also accept one another in His body. In addition, we must forgive and accept those who have hurt and rejected us in the past. To take the love of God out to multitudes suffering from rejection in the world's harvest field requires reapers whose hearts and relationships express God's love and acceptance.

A great strength in body ministry is the diversity with which the Lord has equipped His people. Life comes out of the divine dynamics of interactive relationships. Unfortunately, a common fault for many is to copy or seek to be like someone else—perhaps one who has a more visible or exciting place of ministry. However, such misguided ambition only weakens the body. It is vital to walk only in that to which we have been called in Christ. This calls for humility and sound judgment. At the same time, we are not to stand behind others in the background; each one is to present himself to the Lord for service.

> *For through the grace given to me I say to every man among you not to think more highly of himself than he ought to think; but to think so as to have sound judgment, as God has allotted to each a measure of faith* (Romans 12:3).

The body of Christ is not made up of performers and spectators. Each member has a role to play according to the grace resting upon him. It may not involve public ministry of the word or a place in leadership, but it will be necessary for proper functioning of the body. The most important ministry in a local body is often one that is not highly visible. I suspect that in the final reckoning, prayer and intercession are probably the greatest spheres of service. A key word is diversity!

> *...there are **varieties** of gifts, but the same Spirit. And there are **varieties** of ministries, and the same Lord* (1 Corinthians 12:4-5).

...to each one is given the manifestation of the Spirit for the common good (1 Corinthians 12:7).

The goal is for *each* member to be equipped to serve, for the Lord's work requires His whole body.

As each one has received a special gift, employ it in serving one another, as good stewards of the manifold grace of God (1 Peter 4:10).

Prepared for the Fields

The mission field begins at home. How should a renewed church prepare workers for foreign lands? That primarily will come from the vision, training, and experience gained in home church outreach in their locality. A comprehensive anointed strategy that involves the whole church, with many diverse endeavors, is important.

A good example for churches to emulate is the Hope of Bangkok church in Bangkok, Thailand. In his 1996 Christmas Newsletter, Dr. Joseph Wongsak, founder of Hope of Bangkok, reports that they have now planted 480 churches in that nation. Their goal is to touch every district in Thailand. People are being trained and sent out across the country to discover areas where there is no witness as yet, and to begin church plants. The home church has grown rapidly. There are now 24 worship services a week to allow all the people, including several different language groups, to participate. There are 2,000 group leaders to serve the many who are coming into God's family. The major ministry emphasis by Dr. Wongsak has been to be *salt and light to the community*. To that end, he works with business organizations, the government, seminars, local universities, newspapers, magazines, and television to present Christian values.

In 1996 Hope of Bangkok planted six more churches overseas for a total of 32 in 16 nations. What an excellent testimony of global outreach being developed out of the vision, training, and practice of local church evangelism!

Young people can have their hearts prepared with a burden for the place they will later be sent to. This could begin when they are sent out as part of an apostolic team under adult leadership for short visits to the field. It can be the time when God touches their hearts, and they will never be the same again. I have seen this take place in our youth.

Spiritual warfare is an essential part of evangelism since the purpose of the gospel is to free captives from the domain of darkness and bring them into the kingdom of God's dear Son. The essence of satan's strategy is deception. For this reason, workers must be trained to be strong in the Lord and the power of His might, to not be ignorant of satan's schemes or to depend on intellectual religious knowledge. Prayer and intercession are essential for breaking the powers of darkness in lives.

Workers will encounter two primary spheres of satanic activity wherever they will preach the gospel.

1. Fallen angels have been placed over specific regions and geographic areas on earth as ruling authorities to direct satan's activities of evil in these locations. Part of spiritual warfare is discerning the identity and goal of these territorial spirits and wrestling against them in intercession, prayer, fasting, and worship. These forces can be unique to each field of evangelism (see Eph. 6:12).

2. On earth demons carry out evil activities against individuals apparently as they are directed from above.

Preaching the gospel and casting out demons is spiritual warfare.

Preparation of workers for the field will address more than these two areas of warfare. It will include equipping them with the godly armor that Christ has provided to both protect them from schemes of the devil and to overcome him (see Eph. 6:10-18). This armor involves a righteous lifestyle. Walking in truth and the love of God is to wage war against darkness. On the other hand, one who walks in unrighteousness opens his life up to deception, pain, sorrow, and accumulative hindrances. Whether satan flees when we resist him will depend whether or not we are submitting to God in our lives (see Jas. 4:7).

Dean Sherman, well-known teacher and author on spiritual warfare, makes this statement: "Spiritual warfare is not a fragment of Christianity. It is the whole of the Christian experience. It encompasses everything we do. To be a Christian is to be a spiritual warrior. To be a spiritual warrior is to walk consistently and victoriously through life, with Christ at our side."[8]

A vital weapon of attack is the sword of God's Spirit: His Word. Workers need to know the promises of Scripture, and have faith in the Lord Jesus Christ and what He has promised in His Word. The human mind is a major battleground where satan seeks to build strongholds of deception. The promises of God's Word, along with gifts of the Spirit, are tools workers will be equipped with to destroy these fortresses in the lives of those who receive the gospel (see 2 Cor. 10:3-5). Some examples of such strongholds are pride, unforgiveness, fear, depression, condemnation, pornography, racism, the occult, etc.

A vital aspect of strength in spiritual warfare comes from one's relationship and ministry to the Lord in prayer, intercession, and worship. These have top priority in successful evangelism. It is remarkable that everywhere God has moved in renewal, He has raised up anointed worship leaders and minstrels with new songs of the Spirit that declare His heart and purpose for today. These songs and music in worship bring the presence of God into meetings and moves back the darkness. Taking worship out to the streets is an expression of militant evangelism!

Prepared for Pain

So far we have examined the qualities of character, relationship, and ministry in preparing reapers.

There is an additional area of preparation. They must also be prepared to persevere and endure pain. Pain and suffering are an integral part of any true revival.

A woman has travail when her hour for delivery has come. Afterwards, she no longer remembers the anguish for joy that a child has been born. Similarly, there is always pain associated with giving birth to righteousness. The following are some examples:

❖ The Father experienced pain in His heart when He sent His Son to bear our sins.

❖ Jesus endured the pain of His cross, despising the shame for the joy that was set before Him (see Heb. 12:2).

❖ Paul (and others since then) experienced pain and travail in order to see Christ received and formed within those to whom he preached (see 2 Cor. 11:24-27; Col. 1:24; Gal. 4:19).

❖ Since the sin of Adam, all of creation groans and suffers the pain of childbirth, waiting for its redemption from decay and corruption (see Rom. 8:21-22).

❖ Israel will experience the pain of travail until she turns in faith to her Messiah.

❖ Lastly, the Church faces the pain of childbirth today as she prepares to deliver overcomers for the end-time purposes of God (see Rev. 12:2). The bride faces pain in preparing herself for the glory of God which will arise upon her in the great conflict and harvest that lies ahead. Believers must be prepared to embrace this redemptive pain, which will come from three sources.

1. There will be new levels of tribulation, persecution, and deception from satan. This time of trouble is described in scripture as "the beginnings of birth pangs" (see Mt. 24:8). Martyrdom will be the way of overcoming for some saints (see Rev. 12:11-12).

2. Whether we are saved or not, the way of our flesh is in opposition to the way of the Spirit. Some believers, who judge only with their rational minds, will react against what takes place when the Holy Spirit moves in renewal power. That is especially true if their hearts have grown cold. God may offend the mind to expose what is in hearts. As God renews the church, criticism and opposition will arise from some believers who judge what is taking place from within the theological boundaries of their tradition, rather than from the fruit that results. Although this opposition will be painful, there must be no retaliation (see 1 Pet. 2:20-23). The pain of accusation is to be covered with a spirit of intercession, love, and mercy. This heart attitude will allow the grace of God to open hearts. Groups or individuals that we may have given up on could become the very ones He uses

in the greatest way. Only the Lord knows what is in hearts, and we must commit into His hands all who oppose us.

3. Another source of pain comes from within us. As the Lord opens our hearts and reveals how much He loves us, something takes place. Sins and idols are surfaced; things that must be acknowledged and put away, for they occupy a place in our hearts that belongs to Jesus. Pride, manipulation, control, elitism, insecurity, and unforgiveness are some of these idols. Unfortunately, because it will be painful, some will draw back from repentance. Habit patterns and indulgent lifestyles have allowed these enemies to become woven into our being. They bring a spirit of heaviness and depression that hinder joy and worship. The Lord is anointing His people, doing heart surgery to remove these things and give us the oil of gladness and mantle of praise. However, we must embrace the pain of repentance and forsake those things that God seeks to remove from our lives. It may hurt to do so, but the reward for doing so is great!

The joy of the Lord is our strength; and there is great joy and rejoicing coming in the victories that lie ahead. However, we cannot escape the fire and shaking of the process that takes us there. We must be prepared for pain.

Reapers for Israel

In His purpose for the last days, God has specific callings for individuals, churches, and nations. For example, I believe Canada has a unique calling by God for the last days, one that is different than that of the United States.

However, the nation of Israel occupies a special place among nations. The Lord initially came to Israel as her Messiah to fulfill the Old Covenant, and to make her a blessing to all nations according to His promises to Abraham.

Because Israel did not recognize the day of her visitation she was dispersed as a people among the nations, with only a remnant entering into the New Covenant era of the Church. However, Israel was not cut off from God forever. He promised to regather them to the land and bring salvation to her people.

When God began to renew the Church with the "Latter Rain" revival in 1948, it was only a matter of weeks before Israel became a nation. In the "Charismatic Renewal" of the 1960/70 era, Jerusalem again became part of Israel.

Since 1948, there has been an ever increasing number of Jews returning to the land of Israel. God is bringing them back, even though they are coming with their hearts closed to the knowledge and love of their Messiah.

In concert with this, groups of Messianic believers have sprung up in various lands, Jews who have come to Christ, and whose hearts are stirred up to see the salvation of Israel. Through their outreach there are rapidly increasing numbers of new believers in Messiah. From these bodies, a number of ministries are moving to Israel with a vision to see the redemption of that nation. They are reapers being prepared for Israel (see Ezek. 37:1-10).

Although the details of events that will take place have not been revealed, the Lord does have a strategy of harvest for that land. The following observations and Scriptures provide a rough overview of how His purpose may unfold.[9]

1. Israel is dominated today by secular humanism and demonic religious forces. There is a strong satanic authority over that part of the world; there will be further war and bloodshed, but the heavens are where the real battle must be fought! In His time, the Lord will shake the powers of heaven and bring down this ruler of evil forces. Worshiping our wonderful Lord Jesus in Spirit and in truth drives back darkness over an area. The significance of worship by the body of Christ, when the Lord moves in judgment power against principalities and powers, is pictured for us in the following Scripture:

   *For at the voice of the Lord Assyria will be terrified, when He strikes with the rod. And every blow of the rod of punishment, which the Lord will lay on him, **will be with the music of tambourines and lyres**...* (Isaiah 30:31-32).

   Therefore, spiritual worship and intercession are essential for fruitful evangelism in Israel.

2. Romans 11:23-32. Salvation will come to Israel, but not until the fullness of the Gentiles (i.e., Gentile nations) has come in.

3. Romans 11:11,13-14. A key to Israel's salvation is when they become jealous of what they see God doing in the Church. This will require apostolic men like Paul, with a vision to raise up empowered, vibrant expressions of the body of Messiah that would make the nation jealous. Nominal Messianic church life with Jewish customs, laws, and culture alone will not impress orthodox Jews. They must see the power, love, mercy, and compassion of God demonstrated in the name of Messiah. They must see a reality that only comes from the Holy Spirit.

4. Romans 11:12,15. The fulfillment of Israel's salvation will mean riches to the world, for it will be the final completion of the one new man that God has ordained for His dwelling place among men[10] (see Eph. 2:12-22). Fullness of the Church cannot take place apart from Jewish believers. All Israel will be saved, and the emphasis at that time will not be on Jewish or Gentile churches, but on the "one new man"— on the bride of Messiah! The hearts of His people will then be lifted up from the turmoil of earthly issues in Israel to the city of Messiah, the heavenly Jerusalem, the city of the living God (see Rev. 21:2-3,10-11,22-24). Israel may well have a ministry to nations during the Millennium, one that will be centered in Jerusalem. However, in this age the eyes of God's children do not look for a lasting or permanent city on earth; we seek the city that is to come, the place of destiny for the redeemed (see Heb. 12:22-23; 13:14). There is a blessing inherent today in praying for the salvation of Israel, entreating the Lord to send reapers into that land with a vision to raise up revived, empowered churches to provoke the nation to jealousy.

One cannot prepare reapers for the harvest without also preparing local assemblies to shepherd the fruits of their labor. Let us consider some of the changes facing the Church; for the Church of tomorrow will not be like the Church of today.

Chapter 4

Preparing the Barns

New Wineskins

The Lord is not a husbandman who would send reapers into fields to gather in the harvest without having prepared barns to put the grain in. Neither would He pour out new wine without preparing a wineskin to contain it.

The wind of the Holy Spirit blowing over the land today will not only change hearts, it is also going to affect structures and institutions. A great shaking is coming; everything that can be shaken will be shaken! Nothing will be able to stand other than what God has built (see Heb. 12:25-27). Only what has been birthed in the heart of God will abide for eternity.

Mike Bickle, who is currently Senior Pastor of Metro Christian Fellowship, testifies how God sovereignly spoke to him on September 1982 while he was visiting Cairo, Egypt.

The Holy Spirit clearly said that He was going to change the understanding and expression of Christianity over the entire world in one generation! The way the world views the relevance and expression of Christianity will be totally changed in one generation.

I believe that this process of change has begun. Change, change, and more change! That is what we face in the days ahead.

Personal Renewal—The First Step

A common mind-set says: "If the church would correct its doctrine and government, then renewal of the saints would follow." Such thinking is backwards; the Lord first renews hearts, from which emerge changes in the Church.

Ministers of renewal are to reach out in faith and love to all Christian bodies *just as they are.* The emphasis is not to change externals, but to point individuals to the One who will do so, from the inside out. Once personal renewal comes, the Holy Spirit will change the wineskin.

This chapter examines the early Church for those truths and principles which the Holy Spirit may restore. One thing is certain, renewal and restoration will involve great shaking of the status quo.

A Time of Shaking

Unless the Lord opens our hearts we may not recognize His hand in the traumatic events and shaking that is sure to come. For example, the Israelites in Egypt saw Pharaoh as an enemy to them and to God's purpose. In fact, God had raised Pharaoh up as a vessel through whom to reveal the glory and power of His might in delivering His people from Egypt.

When Arthur Wallis visited China to see the mighty work of God in the underground church there, he found that the Lord had used the Communists much as He had used Pharaoh. The Communists' stand against religion created "a spiritual vacuum" in which a pure church could arise. They were used by God to remove three hindrances: ancestor worship, Buddhism, and the weak foundation that had been laid for Christianity by the missionary groups.

As Wallis states in his book, *China Miracle* (pp. 34-48):

> "The other weakness of the early missionary effort, like that of the Nestorian and Catholic enterprises before it, was that it imposed Western forms of worship and culture upon the Chinese, ways that were totally for-eign to them. Most of the early missionary organiza-tions failed to see that if the church was ever to rest naturally in the soil of china, it needed to be divested of its Western forms. (Hudson Taylor was the exception to this criticism)....Another weakness was that mission-ary organizations generally established their churches on denominational lines...each retaining its own dis-tinctive identity...and its own particular form of church government...."[11] (pp. 34-48)

The long, dark night of communism in China has wit-nessed the birth of perhaps the best example of true Christi-anity on the earth today.

What about the Church in America? It certainly is to be commended for sending the gospel to nations, tribes, and peoples all over the world. God has blessed America because of this; but now an affluent lifestyle, spiritual competition, and worldliness has made many hearts lukewarm. The ministry of God's word has become institutionalized.

As Dr. Michael Brown states in his book *The End of the American Gospel Enterprise*:

> *"...what began as a movement in Jerusalem became a philosophy in Greece, an institution in Rome, a culture in Europe, and an enterprise in America...."*[12]

Church organizations are often more like business enterprises than expressions of the body of Christ. Such an environment does not portray the simplicity, love, and spontaneity of the early Church. When we compare the Church in America to the Church described in the Book of Acts, the need for renewal becomes clear!

How do we begin? Where do we start? First of all, we must seek and obey the Lord. What is He saying? I believe His words are clear; He wants His Church back!

Give Me Back My Church

After all, the Church is His house; it is not ours; and He insists on being Head in what is rightfully His.

Make no mistake about it! Christ Himself, must have center stage! Only to the extent that His Lordship is recognized as more important than all persons, all doctrine, and all tradition, will the Holy Spirit be free to do His work.

Let us use the Scriptures to transport us back in time and view the Church in its divine infancy. It becomes apparent that these early believers were committed to loving and nurturing one another, standing united in their testimony for Christ by a faith that was largely centered in four practices.

> *And they were continually devoting themselves to the* **apostles' teaching**, *and to* **fellowship**, *to the* **breaking of bread** *and to* **prayer** (Acts 2:42).

The credibility of their witness for Christ was expressed in a joyful lifestyle that produced spiritual fruit on a daily basis.

> *And* **day-by-day** *continuing with one mind in the temple, and breaking bread from house to house, they were taking their meals together with gladness and sincerity of heart, praising God, and having favor with all the people. And the Lord was* **adding to their number day-by-day** *those who were being saved* (Acts 2:46-47).

It was not doctrines, practices, or sacraments that bound them together, but the common, living union they had in the Spirit with Christ. Life in Christ cannot be understood by doctrine and definitions; it must be experienced. It is described by the phrase, "to share a common life through the Holy Spirit."

> *But the one who joins himself to the Lord is* **one spirit with Him** (1 Corinthians 6:17).

This life union in the Spirit is what constituted membership in the early Church.

The centrality of Christ to these early saints was not exhibited simply in their admiration of His words and deeds but in their personal obedience to Him. His Lordship was real to them!

There was no concept of two classes of believers (i.e., performers and spectators). The following verse expresses their concept of ministry in a meeting:

What is the outcome then, brethren? When you assemble, **each one** *has a psalm, has a teaching, has a revelation, has a tongue, has an interpretation. Let all things be done for edification* (1 Corinthians 14:26).

Each true believer was an active minister whenever the body of Christ assembled. The Lord Himself was the center of their attention. It was He who they worshipped; it was His words that they sought to hear and obey. And His presence was manifested by daily occurrences of the supernatural in various gifts and ministries.

Equip My Sheep

Whenever the emphasis of a church becomes mired in programs, committees, politics, or organization, such things will inevitably usurp priority over the pre-eminence of Christ. The end result is a stifling of body ministry, and the control of what takes place in the assembly begins to pass from the Holy Spirit into the hands of man.

I recall watching on television the performance of a musician who alternately played a violin or an accordion. At the same time, he accompanied himself with a harmonica held in position by a strap around his head, and he supplied timing for his music by beating a drum with sticks tied to his feet. Although the quality of his music was not great, his ability to simultaneously play several instruments was most impressive.

The musician reminded me of what congregations today demand of their pastor. He is expected to perform all spiritual tasks in the assembly, to represent the church in the local community, and to administrate all major functions for the congregation.

This mind-set is not from God, and it certainly did not exist in the early Church. The Lord sees a local church much like a symphony orchestra. As conductor, He desires to express a harmony of spiritual ministry through the many instruments that He has chosen to make up His body. The skill of any one particular member is not nearly as important as the orchestration of *all* members.

Thus, the ultimate measure of success for leaders in the Church is not in the excellence of their personal performance, but rather, how well they equip and prepare each individual believer to serve. To equip a saint for his place in the body of Christ is to establish what God has planned from eternity for that person. The greatest tragedy in life is not death, but a life lived that failed to find and fulfill the call of God! And the place of equipping is God's seminary, the local church.

It is within the collective relationship of those in union with Christ that each believer finds his identity and place of service. The emphasis is not who we are in Him, but who He is in us. There is a unique deposit of His life within each of us that determines our call and service in His body. He desires to be center focus in *all* things that concern us, so that it is never a question of how much or how little ability we have.

This organism of body life in the early Church was not based on religious organization. It was simply the life union, or spiritual communion, that believers had with Christ and with one another.

Spiritual service is a question of grace and anointing. The Holy Spirit distributes spiritual gifts to each one just as He wills, and God places each member in the body as He desires (see 1 Cor. 12:11,18).

> *...God has so composed the body, giving more abundant honor to that member which lacked that there should be*

no division in the body, but that the members should have the same care for one another (1 Corinthians 12:24-25).

Because God sees us as one body in Christ, we must love all other members regardless of ethnic or other differences. We are called collectively to become an expression of the will and character of Christ. This requires unity. There must be no gossip, division, back-biting or fault-finding. Instead we are to serve, comfort, admonish, love, and care for one another.

The body of Christ is a place of transition where one learns to be less concerned about personal needs and more committed to meet the needs of others. This is the primary motivation of body ministry and outreach in the community.

Therefore encourage one another, and build up one another... (1 Thessalonians 5:11).

And let us consider how to stimulate one another to love and good deeds (Hebrews 10:24).

The dynamics of relationship, outreach, and body ministry are best developed and practiced in small groups, which was why the early Church was built in homes.

In an article entitled, *"The Quest of Kings,"* Rick Joyner makes the following observation: "The failure of the church to understand her own history can be found as one of the main reasons for the shallowness, lack of vision, and the most devastating mistakes of the church today."[13] I agree with this statement. Let us address the issue of lost principles and practices of spiritual life, and how God may restore them as He renews His people.

The Need for Church Renewal

When we consider the power and witness of the first believers, we are faced with the question, "What on earth happened to the Church?" It is easy to blame Church failures and problems on the devil; after all, he is committed to lawlessness while we who believe are on God's side. However, the real culprit is the hand of man!

As institutional control emerged and grew, overruling the Holy Spirit, charismatic gifts of the Holy Spirit diminished, and the Church began its decline into that period of time known as the dark ages. With the reformation, Church restoration began. Since then numerous revivals have occurred in which lost truths were restored. Men and women of the Spirit have been raised up by the Lord as His witnesses, and denominations have emerged from these periods of revival. However, there is still truth to be restored, and God's heart for both Israel and the Church in the last days is restoration in times of refreshing.

> *Repent therefore and return, that your sins may be wiped away, in order that **times of refreshing may come from the presence of the Lord;** and that He may send Jesus, the Christ appointed for you, whom heaven must receive **until the period of restoration of all things** about which God spoke by the mouth of His holy prophets from ancient time* (Acts 3:19-21).

Let us briefly examine areas where too many contemporary churches differ from those in the first century. It is important to recognize that none of the following issues

91

disqualify a church from the grace and renewal power of God. Indeed, they are why renewal is necessary.

1. The early believers came together frequently throughout the week to spontaneously share their life in Christ with one another. They were committed to the process of making disciples for Christ. The church of today gathers once, or perhaps twice, in a week to experience a programmed, one-hour service of song, announcements, and sermon with the hope of gaining decisions for Christ. (I am not suggesting that God doesn't anoint programs.)

2. The first assemblies had no official church buildings for over two hundred years; the saints gathered in homes (see Philem. 1:2; Col. 4:15; Rom. 16:5; Acts 2:46; 20:20). Today a church is largely identified by its building, and in some cases even by the building's architecture. The emphasis today is more on "going to church" than on "being the Church." There is nothing wrong in having a church building; the problem is in the emphasis of large gatherings to the neglect of building bonds of relationship in small group environments.

3. Congregations of believers in the early Church viewed themselves as a local expression of the body of Christ in their city. They were a charismatic body in the Spirit with each believer committed to being a unique contributor of the life of Christ. In contrast, present-day churches are often structured to function as institutions with believers divided into two classes: clergy (performers) and laity (spectators). A church is weakened when believers find it easier to pay someone to do

the work of God rather than face the commitment of obeying His call on their lives.

4. The first Church presented the united witness and testimony of one gospel and one body in Christ to a pagan world. Their message was the gospel of the kingdom of God. Today there are many gospels, such as: fundamentalism, the full gospel, dominion theology, liberation theology, the social gospel, the sacramental liturgical gospel, gospel of faith and prosperity, etc. Although all promise, in some measure, the grace and salvation of God, the gospel of the kingdom is uniquely centered around the government and centrality of Christ in salvation. The proponents of these gospel emphases compete with one another to gain members and influence. They seek to maintain unity within the context of their own denominational body of doctrine and practice. As James Rutz so accurately states in his excellent book *The Open Church*: "We have denominations today that are custom made for thinkers, for feelers, and for doers."[14]

5. The original Church obeyed the Lord's command to avoid titles when referring to their ministries (see Mt. 23:8-12). In contrast, churches today identify their various ministers through titles. (Some examples are: Reverend, Senior Pastor, Archbishop, General Superintendent, Cardinal, Pope, etc.) In the early Church, authority of ministers was evident by the grace and anointing that rested upon them, and was endorsed by their exemplary lifestyle; it was not resident in titles. The use of titles imply a God-given authority. However, for whatever reason, if anointing or godly character is not present in a minister, his title can replace the

authority that comes from the Holy Spirit's anointing in the eyes of the people, which opens the door to be led into error by ungodly men.

6. A characteristic of early Church meetings was "spontaneity." They gathered in excitement and expectancy to worship the Lord and to hear from Him. The acts of the Holy Spirit were present in their midst. They did not come with personal agendas. Contemporary characteristics in some churches today would be "program" and "liturgy," where expectancy is limited to hearing a good sermon and being entertained by the music.

7. Meetings of the early Church were rich in spiritual gifts, ministries, and prayer. The essence of services was the believers' day-by-day testimony of what God was speaking and doing in their midst. Modern-day services are often sermons oriented around definition and doctrine. The emphasis is more on theology, and how God moved in the past, rather than what He is currently speaking.

8. Credibility of the early Church was evident in the power of God, in the accountable relationship and love the members had for one another, and in their godly lives of righteousness. On one occasion, the Lord took the lives of a husband and wife who had sinned in order to preserve the validity of this testimony. Some traditional churches seek credibility through legalism, orthodoxy of creeds, and proper positions on social issues. Unfortunately, credibility of the Church today is often weakened by reports of leaders divorcing and falling into sin, as well as by sectarianism and competition between religious bodies.

The above eight areas provide examples of where we are beginning to see changes, and where we can expect to see much more as the gracious work of renewal and restoration continues. A related area of renewal is that of church leadership, those who will oversee the dynamics of harvest.

Shepherding and Oversight

Multitudes saved in a short time; renewal fires burning in denominations with vastly different models of government and structure; persecution and afflictions; a great need for leaders—these words describe a probable future environment which will give birth to new qualities in leadership.

To anticipate what this might mean, let us examine the apostolic model of leadership in the early church.

The apostles were trained to be bond-servants, and as such, to be examples to all men who would follow them (see Mt. 20:25-28; 2 Tim. 2:24; Tit. 1:1; Jas. 1:1; 2 Pet. 1:1).

When Scripture refers to a local church (i.e., the church at Corinth), it included all believers in that city. These local churches, which may have comprised a large number of assemblies in homes, were shepherded by pastoral teams of men called elders. Oversight was shared among a plural company of these men[15](see Acts 14:23; Tit. 1:5; 1 Pet. 5:1-3). Apostles traveled between cities, laying foundations for new churches, ordaining elders, and strengthening the faith of believers. What did it mean to oversee and shepherd the Lord's sheep in the early Church? It should certainly mean the same today.

A good place to begin is to study the following three commissions to shepherd:

1. The Father commissioned Jesus as the good Shepherd (see Jn. 10:1-18; Ps. 23).

2. Jesus commissions Peter to shepherd His sheep (see Jn. 21:15-17).

3. Peter commissions elders to shepherd the flock of God in their locality (see 1 Pet. 5:1-3).

A shepherd will only love the Lord's sheep to the extent that he loves the Lord. Out of that love, he will feed and nourish the young and the old. He will help the weak and sickly. He will teach them to know the voice of the Lord. He will tend, guide, counsel, and care for them, while guarding them from spiritual wolves and heresy. He will disciple them with patience. Redemptive discipline is also an inherent component of godly oversight. He will do all these things, not for the sake of being paid, but because he loves them enough to lay down his life for them.

However, there is more to shepherding. How does one reconcile the above responsibilities of shepherding with the commission that the five ministries of Ephesians 4:11-13 have to equip the sheep for their work of service?

The issue to be faced is this: "How can elders oversee, feed, guard, care for, disciple, and lead the flock of God if another group of men (apostles, prophets, evangelists, pastors, and teacher) are to equip them for service?" One cannot be equipped to minister in a spiritual vocation apart from also being equipped with the character to do so. It becomes apparent that the equipping process is inherently an integral part of shepherding. The two functions *cannot* be separated! Elders must be both shepherds and equippers; they should be men with an ascension gift ministry.

In the early Church, Peter was an elder as well as apostle at Jerusalem; and apparently, Judas and Silas were also elders as well as prophets at the same church (see Acts 15:22,32).

Why is diversity so important in church oversight? One reason is that both internal (local) life as well as outreach (translocal) life are at stake.

✤ Pastors are needed to care for the saints, and to teach and equip them by example, to care for, admonish, and love them.

✤ Teachers are necessary so that the saints are taught about the Lord and His ways, and are equipped to instruct, encourage, and edify each other.

✤ Evangelists impart the Lord's heart of compassion for the lost and equip the saints to evangelize.

✤ Prophets have grace to hear and express the heart of God to individuals, congregations, and nations. The grace upon them equips the saints to be a prophetic people in the Lord. Their messages will be used to ignite prayer and intercession on issues that are vital to bring God's visitations and purpose to fruition.

✤ The glory of tomorrow arises out of the vision that God is bringing today. Where there is no vision for restoration, the tradition of men will prevail. Apostles have grace to see the whole picture. Scripture is clear that to attain unity of the faith and the maturity belonging to the fullness of Christ, the Church requires the ministry of apostles as well as prophets, pastors, teachers, and evangelists (see Eph. 4:11-13). For this reason, we can expect to see ministers emerge who will be recognized as apostles. The pastor-led, episcopal structure of traditional churches makes such recognition difficult, but restoration is inevitable. The foundational nature of this ministry, in concert with prophets, is necessary to unite and strengthen churches in the purpose of God for this hour. When renewal or revival breaks out in an area, there is generally one whom God will use to lead or father what He is doing. Such men have apostolic grace to show the way and be a model to local churches. The following are some of the qualities and ministry functions that one would expect such men to exhibit.[16,17]

Apostolic Ministry

True apostles would not see themselves as greater than other ministries, only different because of the grace of their calling (see 1 Cor. 15:10; Eph. 4:7). Their authority would be resident and evident in their anointing and godly character, not in titles or offices.

In stewardship they would be bond-servants who lead and motivate others by example. Their emphasis in ministry would be to see believers conformed to the image of Christ and body life in the Spirit restored to churches. They would not build personal kingdoms around their ministries. Their whole focus would be Jesus!

They would be apostles of Christ, not apostles of a denomination, even though that could be their background. They would promote unity, power, and godliness in and between churches within the sphere of their service, and their geographic spheres of ministry could be quite different (see 2 Cor. 10:13-16).

They would not be dictatorial or dominate local church leadership, but would interface with them on a relational basis in the love of God. They would encourage leaders to unite for prayer, worship, and evangelism.[18]

Paul used the word "master-builder" to describe his apostolic ministry (see 1 Cor. 3:10). This word is translated from a Greek word *Achitekton*, which literally means "beginning craftsman." Thus apostles understand the foundation principles in planting churches.

I work with several ministers across the land who, although not generally recognized as apostles, have this ministry.

It can be frustrating to possess God's call and anointing of a prophet or an apostle, but be constrained by demands to fulfill the traditional role of church pastor.

Developing Leaders

Servants. All ministry in a church begins here: hearts seeking to serve others in response to the love they have experienced in Christ. God calls all of His children to be servants; from servants He chooses leaders—not leaders who serve, but servants who lead by example. Men who exercise the gentle authority of servanthood are men to whom He will entrust His sheep.[19]

Any ministry to which God calls a man to serve has both a grace and a sphere associated with it. If one proves faithful and fruitful in his sphere, God may, in time, extend grace for a larger dimension of service. Of course, the first sphere is always one's own family. To assume a wider sphere, without God's grace to do so, can lead to failure. What one builds in ministry he can destroy by sin or cripple by presumption. Thus, the condition of one's heart is always vitally important since public ministry is an expression of his personal life.

The systemic training of a Bible school or seminary is valuable. However, such facilities may not always be available in the future. The local church was God's seminary in the beginning. If we understand how men were trained for eldership in the early Church, we can see more clearly how the Lord may restore this aspect of His Church, and what should be emphasized in the equipping process.

Paul spent three years at Ephesus training men to become elders. He later returned to Ephesus, and calling the elders together, he reviewed his training syllabus and the examples he had set for them to follow (see Acts 20:17-38). The following are the highlights and emphases of his review:

❖ He reminded them of his humility and faithfulness during the trials and persecution he faced while with them (verses 18-19).

❖ He taught the whole purpose of God, not simply basic salvation and evangelism (verse 27).

❖ He taught and practiced a total commitment to the grace of God, to His kingdom and to evangelism (verses 21, 24-25).

❖ He taught them in public, central meetings, as well as in house churches (verse 20).

❖ He reminded them how he had supported himself by secular work, demonstrating that his goal in ministry was not material gain. He was also able to financially help others, and made it clear to the elders that, in doing so, he had set an example for them to follow (verses 33-35).

❖ He stressed the importance of their service as overseers, reminding them of how he had repeatedly warned them with tears to constantly guard their hearts against pride and to stand together in caring for the flock (verses 28-31).

❖ That he had established a good relationship with these men during the training period appears evident from verses 37 and 38.

It would appear that the church at Ephesus was destined to have a good eldership, considering the excellence of Paul's training program, and recognizing that men appointed as elders would meet all the qualifications that he himself had set down in epistles to Timothy and Titus (see 1 Tim. 3:1-7; Tit. 1:5-9). However, such was not the case. After Paul left, certain elders began to bring forth perverse teaching to draw away disciples after them (see Acts 20:29-30).

It is evident that training and qualities at ordination are not sufficient. It is also necessary for leaders to continually guard their hearts from pride, being open to corrective input directly from the Holy Spirit, or as He would speak to them through their peers. The following qualities are necessary for shared leadership to be successful: *commitment to Christ's headship, transparency with accountability, fervent love for one another, humility, and forbearance.*

It is possible there may be instances when the harvest will be so vast and sudden that there will not be time to train qualified elders. At such times, God may sovereignly anoint relatively new converts, if they are humble and lowly in heart, to provide leadership.

Potential leaders are not always obvious. Many from the "flower children/hippie" culture of that day, who were saved in our meetings during the charismatic renewal, are now church leaders.

Spiritual Authority in the Church

There is an implicit authority in any ministry anointed by the Holy Spirit. This will vary according to ministry function; for example, the authority of an apostle is different from that of an evangelist.

The issue is not whether we have sufficient authority for the task God has called us to, but rather, how we are to conduct ourselves so that the authority of our ministry is received. Authority has no value if it is not accepted by those whom it is to serve. Overseers must shepherd the flock of God in such a manner that the authority of their oversight will be received by the sheep.

We are given an excellent example of how to do this by Paul's ministry at Thessalonica. In his epistle to this church, Paul reviews how he had conducted himself so that this particular assembly would recognize and accept his apostolic authority (see 1 Thess. 2:1-13). Actually, Paul's task was probably twofold: to establish foundations of the church, and at the same time, to mentor the two younger apostles who accompanied him (see 1 Thess. 1:1; 2:6). The truths he presents provide good instruction for all ministers. The following review reveals the supreme importance Paul placed on godly character in relationship to his authority in the church:

❖ He avoided all appearance and acts of greed (verse 5).

❖ He did not flatter the people or seek honor because of his ministry reputation (verses 5 and 6).

❖ He was gentle with the people, much like a nursing mother would care for her child (verse 7).

❖ He supported himself by secular work, laboring night and day in order to preach the gospel without charge (verse 9).

❖ He lived a devout, blameless, and exemplary life before the people whom he taught (verses 8 and 10).

❖ He exhorted, implored, and encouraged the saints much as a father would his own children (verse 11).

Paul thanked God that because of the humility and commitment he had demonstrated in serving the people, they recognized his apostolic ministry by receiving his words as the word of God!

Paul's example provides a godly pattern for how to exercise the authority of oversight. No one should assume his authority will be received simply because he bears a title or occupies an office.

Worthy Men

An important part of the Lord's ministry on earth was training the 12 apostles for their future work in building the Church.

After a period of appropriate teaching, Jesus sent them to preach the gospel of the kingdom to the nation of Israel. They were commanded to preach, heal the sick, cleanse the lepers, and cast out demons. They were also given an important, specific instruction concerning each locality they ministered in.

> *And into whatever city or village you enter, inquire **who is worthy** in it; and abide there until you go away. And as you enter the house, give it your greeting. And if **the***

103

house is worthy, *let your greeting of peace come upon it...* (Matthew 10:11-13).

The Greek word translated as "worthy" is *Axios*, from which our English word "axle" is derived.

The essence of Jesus' direction to them was clear. The first step before ministering in any village or city was to locate a worthy man there, whose home (family) life was also worthy—that is, one whose reputation made him and his house a center of influence for good in the community, a "weight bearing" center for moral good among the populace. The proclamation of the gospel was to be associated with this godly man and his home.

When the Holy Spirit fell, and the Church was birthed on the day of Pentecost, the apostles continued to practice this principle as the early Church was built in homes. Evangelism took place in the synagogues, but homes were where the Church was built. The family is God's nuclear unit for building His Church, and house churches provide an excellent informal environment to win and disciple adults and children in Christ. The character requirements for elders of these early churches qualified them as being worthy men (see 1 Tim. 3:2-7; Tit. 1:5-9).

As the fire of God touches cities, and great revival breaks out with hundreds and even thousands being saved, the most immediate need is not bigger church buildings; rather, it will be for worthy homes overseen by worthy men where converts can be established in Christ. There is essentially no way to estimate the number of homes in a populated area that may become available when God moves in power. What will be needed is leaders with wisdom and anointing to shepherd these homes.

Shepherding Young Warriors

There are marvelous reports from various places of the Spirit of God moving upon children. Visions, words of knowledge, healings, prophecy, and adults being "slain in the Spirit" as children lay hands upon them! A new "breed" of youth will be supernaturally raised up, who will not fit today's stereotype of Sunday school.

We should expect this to take place if we are indeed in the time of God's visitation. He has declared in His Word, that in the day of His power at the end of this age, there would be a special anointing upon the youth.

> *...I will pour out My Spirit on all mankind; and your **sons** and your **daughters** will prophesy...your **young men** will see visions...* (Joel 2:28).

> *...Your people will offer themselves willingly in the day of your power, in the beauty of holiness and in holy array out of the womb of the morning; **to You will spring forth Your young men who are as the dew*** (Psalm 110:3 AMP).

The RSV translation of this verse is as follows:

> *...Your people will offer themselves freely on the day You lead Your host...from the womb of the morning like dew **Your youth will come to You**.*

The issue to be faced is how to prepare, shepherd and equip the children. Because of the Lord's sovereign grace in the coming days of harvest, there will be some young people saved whom the Lord will quickly bring forth into His service, much as He called Jeremiah to be a prophet (see Jer. 1:6-10). However, this will not be the norm; parents and church leaders are responsible to equip and prepare their youth for the time ahead. The Lord specifically addresses this preparation through the prophet Malachi:

> *Behold, I am going to send you **Elijah** the prophet before the coming of the great and terrible day of the Lord. And he will **restore** the hearts of the fathers to their (the) children, and the hearts of the children to their fathers, lest I come and smite the land with a curse* (Malachi 4:5-6).

The spirit of Elijah that rested upon John the Baptist was an *essential* requirement for the Lord's first coming. John's ministry prepared the way of the Lord. The spirit of Elijah is also necessary to restore and prepare the Church for His second coming. This spirit is the basis of spiritual restoration, and it concerns the relationship of fathers to their children, both in a natural and spiritual sense.

> *And His disciples asked Him, saying, "Why then do the scribes say that Elijah must come first?" And He answered and said, "Elijah is coming and **will restore all things**...* (Matthew 17:10-11).

The greatest miracle Elijah accomplished took place during the years when he built into Elisha the truths he had learned and the spiritual ministry that God had developed in him. He ministered to Elisha as to a son. After this time of discipling, when Elisha came forth as a prophet under the anointing and mantle that had rested upon his mentor, he demonstrated a greater excellence of ministry by performing twice as many miracles as Elijah, and he did so without the character flaws of his spiritual father (i.e., fear of Jezebel and self-pity). This is the principle of restoration and equipping that fathers and leaders are to embrace in training today's children.

Unless fathers have hearts to mentor sons who excel them in spiritual stature and excellence of ministry, Church restoration cannot be completed. Just as early Church history was a picture of declension in spiritual qualities, today's generations must experience a spiritual ascension, where what was lost in earlier generations will be restored. Wisdom of age knit with the zeal of youth!

Church leaders of the past were responsible for the falling away, and spiritual fathers today bear responsibility to lead the way in restoration. They require the spirit of Elijah to rest upon them, as it did upon John the Baptist, in order to accomplish the task.

Clearly, fathers must do more than verbally instruct the young. It has been said that one who only *hears* truth will forget; one who *sees* truth in action will remember it; but one who obeys truth will understand and possess it. Thus fathers in the church are to *teach* the young, while *being an example* of what they teach and *participating with* them in ministry. This is the process of mentoring.

A righteous man who walks in his integrity—how blessed are his sons after him (Proverbs 20:7).

Children must know that they are loved to be secure in their relationship with adults. As much as possible, the older children should be present with the adults in renewal meetings.

I believe the trends toward homeschooling and house churches are God-ordained to provide proper environments to train children in the ways of the Lord.

The transition to participating in body ministry with adults in the central meetings is often difficult for young believers. This is made easier if they participate in home church meetings. Because the crowd is smaller, and the format more informal, the atmosphere in home meetings is less likely to make younger members self-conscious.

Young people should not be viewed as "second class" members of the church, but be honored as a specific and important part of the body of Christ. It is often little things that show honor. For example, referring to them as "young adults" rather than "teenagers." Another example would be providing resources for seminars and retreats with youth from other assemblies.

Oversight of youth meetings should be sensitive to how the Holy Spirit would move, rather than following a fixed format, so that they can learn to hear and respond to the voice of the Lord in spiritual gifts. Where possible, and when appropriate, leadership input should come from the more mature of the youth. As the older youth respond to the Lord they become role models for the young ones to emulate.

Parents ought to teach their children in early childhood that an angel of the Lord is always near to protect them. Once they have this knowledge, the Lord may open their eyes to see the angel. This reinforces their faith in the Lord's care for them, and also prepares them for the possible ministry of angels in their later years of serving the Lord. Each major historical period of God's dealings with His people is marked by the ministry of angels. I expect the closing years of this age of grace to experience the greatest manifestation of angelic ministry ever seen in the Church.

The Spirit of Jezebel

Satan has place certain fallen angels as authorities of darkness over populated cities, regions, and countries.

Operating through demons, these principalities exercise specific roles of wickedness in deception and warfare against mankind. The spirit of Jezebel, one of these spirit beings, is the most dominant authority of evil over our nation today![20,21] Church leaders must be able to recognize and know how to deal with this emissary of evil.

Satan has some understanding of the important place children of today will have in the army of the Lord. For this reason, he has a strategy that is directed against them, their families, and the church. The following are three areas of his attack that is woven into the New Age Movement:

✤ To destroy the children through abortion, divorce, pornography, drugs, and the occult.

✤ To destroy male leadership in marriages, and fatherhood in families.

✤ To destroy male leadership in the church. Primary qualifications of elders are largely defined by specific qualities of their family and home lives (see 1 Tim. 3:1-6; Tit. 1:5-9). God always refers to Himself by masculine terms; He is our Father, not our Mother; He is our King, not our Queen. So long as we are in fleshly bodies God has ordained male leadership in the family and church in order to prevent Satan from perverting His headship.

Satan's attack on male leadership is led by demonic spirits that seek to manipulate and control men (often using women). Such spirits are behind the Pro-Choice and Feminist movements. They are also back of homosexuality, "gay rights," and other perversions of the sexes. It is interesting that in satan's kingdom of darkness, witches are over warlocks in covens.

The following are manifestations of this spirit which were apparent in the demonic behavior of Queen Jezebel, who it controlled. The wicked acts of the queen is why this being is called the spirit of Jezebel. Each characteristic represents a unique demonic influence which continues to mark this spirit today.

❖ It is a spirit that seeks to control men and women, but *primarily women,* and to manipulate others through them, often through sexual means. Jezebel fed 400 prophets of the Asherah (a wooden symbol of a female deity) at her table. Her pagan religion included the practice of fertility rites. Besides having a devastating debasing effect on the practitioner, the acts of worship included male and female cultic prostitutes in hetero- and homosexual liaisons. Such corrupt practices as child sacrifice and licentious worship also marked religious devotion to Baal whom Jezebel served.

❖ It is a controlling, rebellious spirit that resists all law and godly authority, especially male authority. Although Ahab, her husband, was king over Israel, it was really Jezebel who ruled. She, not Ahab, defined and led the retaliation against Elijah (see 1 Kings 19:2).

❖ It is a lying, accusing, manipulating spirit. Jezebel manipulated men of authority to have the man Naboth falsely accused and then stoned to death, in order to steal a vineyard he owned.

❖ It is a spirit of devastating fear and discouragement. After Elijah slew the prophets of Baal, demons of fear and discouragement troubled him greatly, so much so that he wanted to die (see 1 Kings 19:3-4).

❖ It is a spirit of witchcraft and the occult. Jezebel served Baal and supported 450 of his demonic prophets. She was instrumental in leading the nation of Israel into idolatry.

❖ It is a spirit of murder and hatred for the word of God. Jezebel destroyed the Lord's prophets in Israel (see 1 Kings 18:4), and she tried to kill Elijah. She played the role of chief priestess to the Baal of that area (Melkarth), a god that required the burning of innocent children as oblations on his altar.

This spirit has been in the world for centuries, but in the strategy of satan, it has been placed over this nation in recent years to bring about the same breakdown in morals that it accomplished over Israel in the days of Ahab and Jezebel. His primary emphasis is to destroy the family unit. The controlling, dominating spirit of Jezebel is the very antithesis of meekness and submission which are the qualities of godly women.

The following are examples and consequences of the works of the "Jezebel spirit" in our nation:

❖ The high and increasing divorce rate.

❖ The Feminist movement.

❖ The current growth of abortions, and the related "Pro-Choice" movement among women.

❖ The permissive lifestyle and philosophy of "if it feels right, do it," and the corresponding growth of drug abuse and premarital sex.

❖ The prominent place of women in the leadership of religious cults (i.e., Christian Science, Unity, Theosophy, and Astrology), and as mediums in channeling within the New Age Movement.

❖ Promoting homosexuality as a permissive lifestyle in society.

The following are examples of subtle overtures in how this spirit can influence leaders in order to destroy or manipulate God's authority in group relationships:

❖ "Your church is the most spiritual and the only right one; don't associate with leaders of other churches."

❖ "You do not have to be accountable to other men; you alone are the leader of the church." (Lack of accountability is a *major* reason why many leaders fall into sin and their ministry is discredited.)

❖ Unexpected and overwhelming spirits of fear or discouragement.

❖ Desires for sexual fantasies.

❖ "The elders lack spiritual insight and wisdom; they are unable to give you counsel, so just ignore their words."

❖ "This renewal is not from God. You will lose control of the church if you embrace it."

God's heart in renewal is to bring all members of His body, including women and children, into their anointed ministries. I expect the Holy Spirit to show no partiality between men, women, and children as He anoints believers for the harvest. However, we must understand the strategies that are back of spiritual warfare today. The second conflict between "Elijah" and "Jezebel" is about to begin! The Lord is apprehending a new generation of fathers with hearts to raise up overcomers, to build the army of the Lord, and to prepare the Church for His return. The spirit of Elijah will rest upon these fathers to bring forth end-time "Elishas."

The final victory over Jezebel did not occur in the days of Elijah. It took place during the lifetime of Elisha, when Jehu was king over Israel. In the final spiritual conflict of this age, the Lord's army, who has been trained by godly fathers with the spirit of Elijah, will see this spirit brought down. The victory will be theirs!

That They May All Be One

What do you think? Would Jesus pray earnestly to His Father for something to take place, that He had been sent to earth to accomplish, and for which He was about to lay down His life, and then not have His prayer answered? Never! One thing is certain, the prayer of our Lord, recorded in John 17, will be answered before He returns. It is an essential part of Church restoration.

> *That they may all be one; even as Thou, Father, art in Me, and I in Thee, that they also may be in Us; that the world may believe that Thou didst send Me* (John 17:21).

Signs and wonders, cell groups, apostles and prophets are not enough. The Lord will not release the fullness of His authority and power to a church that is not united in Him and His purpose. Unity is essential for the spiritual warfare and harvest that lies ahead.

As the spirit of renewal sweeps the Church, the reality of how deeply our Father loves us, just as we are, is changing hearts—not only is our relationship with Him deepening, but we also find ourselves more in love with all of His family. Where doctrinal position and methods were important before, they now seem less important than our love for one another. One of the evident marks of God's grace and sovereignty in places where renewal has broken out (such as Pensacola and Toronto) is how quickly denominational boundaries disappear. Pentecostal, Episcopal, Baptist, Presbyterian, Mennonite, Nazarene, etc., all flowing together in the blessed presence of God's Holy Spirit.

There will never be glory upon the Church apart from unity; and since we are destined for glory, we need to understand the heart of God concerning unity for these days of harvest. To start, let us consider the theology of unity from God's viewpoint, rather than the factors we customarily emphasize.

God's Bridge

God has built a bridge of truth to reach between the hearts of men and churches. It is a bridge that will carry believers over barriers which men have erected. This bridge has great strength and cannot be destroyed. It is supported on four giant pillars of truth that have sovereignly been placed by God Himself. Man had no part in their construction; we are responsible to recognize these truths and walk in obedience to them. The following are these four pillars of truth:

1. Who we belong to and who keeps us. We are united in our family identity; we are kept in one name.

   And I am no more in the world; and yet they themselves are in the world, and I come to Thee. Holy Father, **keep them in Thy name, the name which Thou hast given Me, that they may be one,** *even as We are* (John 17:11).

   There is one God and Father of all, who is over all and through all and in all (Ephesians 4:6).

   Believers are a covenant family; we have one Father, and there is only one name under Heaven given for our salvation. We are redeemed in that name, kept in that name, and all that we do in service for Him is to be done in His name (see Col. 3:17). God has highly exalted the Lord Jesus Christ and bestowed upon Him the name which is above every name; the authority of the Godhead has been invested in His name.

2. What we have become in Christ.

> *For by* **one Spirit** *we were all baptized into* **one body**...*and we were all made to drink of one Spirit* (1 Corinthians 12:13).

> *Now you are Christ's body, and individually members of it* (1 Corinthians 12:27).

It is very simple; all who belong to Christ are collectively one spiritual body, and individually members one of one another. We are spiritually one new man in Christ!

3. Who God has placed over us.

> **One Lord**, *one faith, one baptism* (Ephesians 4:5).

> *And He put* **all** *things in subjection* **under His feet**, *and gave Him as* **head** *over* **all** *things to the church, which is His body, the fulness of Him who fills all in all* (Ephesians 1:22-23).

A living organism can only have one head. Our Lord and Head is Jesus!

4. What God has personally given to us that we may be one and live as one in Him.

> *And the glory which Thou hast given Me I have given to them;* **that they may be one**, *just as we are one; I in them, and Thou in Me that they may be perfected in unity...* (John 17:22-23).

The glory of God is His character or His nature. This is evident from God's answer to Moses who asked to see His glory (see Ex. 33:18-19; 34:6-7). God placed Moses in the cleft of a rock and passed by him in glory declaring the qualities of His person (compassionate, gracious, slow to anger, abounding in lovingkindness and truth, one who keeps lovingkindness for thousands, who forgives iniquity, transgression, and sin, and yet one who preserves justice). Very simply, there is perfect unity in the Godhead; and the same unity will be present among believers who have been conformed into the image or character of Jesus. The glory of God represents qualities that bind believers together in unity.

Christ in us is our hope of glory. We can never reform ourselves enough to produce unity. The life and nature of Christ Himself in our hearts will bond our relationships with one another.

When the world sees how much we love one another, they will believe our message!

Where Does the Bridge Lead?

*You are called in **one hope of your calling*** (Ephesians 4:4).

God has a purpose that He is bringing to completion, one that He set in place before creation. This bridge leads toward the fulfillment of that purpose. Each believer, foreknown by the Lord, has been called and given grace to fulfill a unique role of service in His purpose.

Who has saved us, and called us with a holy calling, not according to our works, but according to His own purpose and grace which was granted to us from all eternity (2 Timothy 1:9).

We can fulfill our calling as we remain on this bridge of unity. We need others to help us. The purpose of God, and our unique place in it, will be fulfilled through the Lord's anointing on each member of His body. Problems, circumstances, business associates, persecution, friends, distresses, brothers and sisters in Christ, are all used by God to work together for our good and help us to fulfill His call on our lives (see Rom. 8:28-32).

How Should We Walk on This Bridge?

The wind of His Spirit comes to shake us, the rain of His Spirit, to refresh us, and the fire of His Spirit, to purge us! All these work together to unite our hearts and purify us from a narrow "party spirit."

Five specific commands instruct us how to walk worthy of our calling. Let us examine each one:

1. We have been saved from sin; thus to walk worthy of our calling, we must be free from the practice and condemnation of sin.

   ...if we walk in the light as He Himself is in the light, we have fellowship with one another, and the blood of Jesus His Son cleanses us from all sin (1 John 1:7).

   There can be no unity where lawlessness and the practice of sin exists.

2. *...walk with all humility and gentleness, with **patience**...* (Ephesians 4:2).

   The body of Christ is made up of members whose abilities, personalities, and ministry graces are all diverse; in addition, each member is imperfect. The Lord commands us to accept one another while recognizing these differences.

   Wherefore, accept one another, just as Christ also accepted us to the glory of God (Romans 15:7).

117

However, it is difficult to receive from others if we only see their imperfections or how they differ from us. For this reason, we must cultivate humility, gentleness, and patience in order to walk together in unity.

Do nothing from selfishness or empty conceit, but with **humility** *of mind* **let each one of you regard one another as more important than himself** (Philippians 2:3).

Vanity and self-importance will disappear when hearts are melted by His love. Being right will not be as important as walking in the love of God.

There is no place for unforgiveness, elitism, racism, or sectarianism.

3. *Showing* **forbearance** *to one another in* **love**... (Ephesians 4:2).

The word *forbearance*, means to control oneself when provoked, "to hold oneself back," or to "refrain from enforcement." It speaks of restraint and patience. In practical terms, God's love prompts us to forgive others, to not speak evil of them or judge them on non-essential issues (i.e., food).

When a believer stumbles in his walk, so often the attitude of other Christians is to expose and condemn rather than to restore the individual. It has been said that the Christian army is the only one that kills its wounded.

Brethren, even if a man is caught in any trespass, you who are spiritual, restore such a one in a spirit of gentleness; each one looking to yourself, lest you too be tempted (Galatians 6:1).

Above all, keep fervent in your love for one another, because love covers a multitude of sins (1 Peter 4:8).

4. *Being diligent to **preserve the unity of the Spirit** in the bond of peace* (Ephesians 4:3).

He who joins himself to the Lord is one spirit with Him (see 1 Cor. 6:17). Since each of us are in union to our Lord by the same Spirit, it is clear that, as we allow Him to rule in our hearts, we can walk in unity with one another in spite of our diversity.

And beyond all these things put on love, which is the perfect bond of unity. And let the peace of Christ rule in your hearts, to which indeed you were called in one body; and be thankful (Colossians 3:14-15).

5. *And He gave some as **apostles**, and some as **prophets**, and some as **evangelists**, and some as **pastors** and **teachers**, for the equipping of the saints for the work of service, to the building up of the body of Christ; **until we all attain to the unity of the faith**, and of the knowledge of the Son of God, to a mature man, to the measure of the stature which belongs to the fulness of Christ* (Ephesians 4:11-13).

While each of us are responsible to preserve unity of the Spirit in the bonds of God's peace, the above Scripture points to an additional responsibility of leaders. They are to see their need for each other in building up the body of Christ to maturity in spiritual stature and to the unity of the faith, which is the ultimate goal of walking worthy in Christ. This can only take place when leaders recognize the need that they and their church have for the grace and anointing of other ministries. No one minister can fully equip the sheep he is responsible to oversee. Unity in the faith is not cheap, for it will require humility and faith to break down barriers of prejudice and embrace the input of others.

In the February 1996 issue of *Spread the Fire*, John Arnott reports that the Toronto church has been networking local pastors since the renewal began. They now have 450 leaders from Toronto and southern Ontario who meet weekly for prayer, mutual support, and exchange of ideas and blessing, as well as ministry to one another. And this networking is growing in scope!

The following are some practical issues that must be faced by leaders in a locality.

❖ Prayer! Leaders praying together is the first step. This must become a priority. It is important to recognize that satan's greatest threat against the Church is as the accuser of the brethren. He will seek to discredit a united testimony for Christ in the area. Unity in the body of Christ must begin with the leaders.

❖ When there is competition between leaders, it is often a sign of uncertainty and insecurity in God's calling. Each one must resolve this issue: A pastor is not an apostle nor is a prophet an evangelist. A servant of the Lord should not compare himself with other ministers, but be concerned with fulfilling his call in God. The Lord has given all five ministries to His whole body, not to just one denomination.

❖ In churches with an inadequacy of ministerial resources to properly equip the saints, the answer can lie in the spiritual resources of neighboring churches. It is not only a good testimony, but there can also be great strength when leaders humble themselves to draw from the life in other assemblies.

❖ Spiritual warfare, persecution, and economic pressures, along with other influences of world darkness, create stress and tension in the lives of believers, which in turn, can give rise to crippling mental or physical infirmities. This will be especially true for leaders in the days ahead. The solution is the peace of God. The most important remedy is a strong personal intimacy with the Lord. However, because of their many responsibilities, leaders also need prayers and words of encouragement from their peers. Satan will seek out the weakest one to destroy the work of God. For that reason, it is important for leaders, as they pray together, to be open, honest, and vulnerable in their relationship with one another, so that they can effectively help bear each other's burden.

❖ As leaders pray together, trust and relationship will be established in their hearts for one another. In time, they will begin to see themselves as an eldership for their locality.[22]

❖ In contending for the truth, leaders must be careful to not equate their understanding of the word with the Word itself. Doctrinal positions can be divisive and intolerant. Truth is not expressed so much in doctrinal statements as it is in how it is walked out in conduct. "Being right" is an attitude that will disappear when we intercede and pray for those who disagree with us. Differences will become lost in the love of God as He renews His Church. The Lord's prayer, *"that they may all be one,"* is going to be answered!

The Dead Church Syndrome

There will probably be some hungry Christians reading these pages who find themselves in a "dead church," where there is no apparent desire for renewal. Everything is driven by "business-as-usual" programs designed to run the church in maintenance mode.

A church member who has this problem, immediately faces the question, "What on earth can, or should, I do about it?" The truth is that there is much that one person can accomplish; he can become an instrument for change in the hand of God. Furthermore, one does not have to be a great student of the Bible or a gifted speaker to do so.

The following are attitudes and actions that **must be avoided**:

- ❖ Criticize the leadership
- ❖ Reorganize the church
- ❖ Go searching for a "perfect church"
- ❖ Fire the pastor
- ❖ Start a new denomination
- ❖ Stop going to church

The place to begin is not the church, but to deal with the reality of where he (or she) is in his relationship to Christ. Personal sin must be repented of and forsaken. All that one needs for a life of victory is available in the cross of Christ.

The second step, if married, is to accept spiritual responsibility toward one's spouse and children as commanded in the Word of God. A church will be no stronger in God than its families are.

The third step is to develop a godly heart attitude toward the people and the leaders of the church.

Until these three issues are faced, one should not be overly concerned about other weaknesses that may be evident in the church. It is possible at this time that the Lord may open the way to attend a new community of believers. Wherever one fellowships, the fourth step lies clearly ahead. One must not gossip or find fault, but rather intercede for the church and its leaders. Prayer and fasting is an ultimate step of becoming real before God. Religion makes people weird, but Jesus makes them real, and spiritual reality is birthed in intercession!

The emphasis is to pray for the Spirit of God to touch hearts bringing renewal and restoration. The best environment for prayer is private gatherings. God's heart is inclusive of all His people, thus prayers should not be limited to only leaders and believers in the assembly, but also include other fellowships in the area. If possible, one should go to a church where the fire of renewal is burning, and bring it back to share with others in the prayer group.

Is it possible that these four steps can transform an inflexible, traditional church into the reality of a living vibrant expression of Christ's body? Before we say, "no way," we should recognize how quickly the Lord moved in response to prayer and brought down communism in Europe. Which is more difficult for Him: to turn a Communist nation into a democracy, or to change a traditional church into a pliable wineskin full of new wine?

We Christians seem to always underestimate the power and sovereignty of God. He *never* leaves His throne, and *nothing* takes place apart from His permissive or directive will! The initiative for renewal and restoration always begins with Him. And where sin is great, the grace of God will abound!

He raises up leaders and nations, and He brings them low according to His will. In the end, all events are simply part of a process in which God will establish His kingdom on earth as it is in Heaven. Nothing is ever beyond the jurisdiction of His authority.

His intent toward us is for good, not evil. His Father heart is a heart of love that wants to change us, to transform us into a victorious people who live above sin and failure; a people who will walk in the provisions of the cross. He is concerned about every area of our lives, no matter how small or insignificant it may be to us. He does not separate our lives into secular and spiritual realms; all that we are and do concern Him. Furthermore, He has no favorite denomination. He loves all of His kids!

In Review

The Lord is calling His people to repent and separate themselves wholly unto Him. He is at work to unite and prepare the Church for a great end-time conflict of spiritual warfare and harvest that brings this age of grace to a close. He is building barns to put the grain in, and we are the material for those barns. The issue we all face is whether we will humble ourselves and submit to His will, or follow our own agenda. There is no place for neutrality. Those who respond in obedience will rule and reign with Him in eternity.

The issue facing us is not one of "going to Heaven"; it concerns the glory that is promised to those who overcome. To go our own way is to forfeit this honor.

Let us next examine the glory of His presence that will rise upon believers in the time of harvest. His glory cannot be separated from the process or the fruits of harvest. The Lord of glory is also the Lord of harvest, and the gospel of His kingdom reveals His glory.

> *Then the glory of the Lord will be revealed, and all flesh will see it together...* (Isaiah 40:5).

This will also be the time when the church prepares for the glory of His return in the clouds of heaven; which, in turn, will lead to His ultimate goal to fill the earth with the knowledge of His glory as the waters cover the sea (see Hab. 2:14).

Chapter 5

The Glory of His Presence

The Horizon of Glory

The far horizon of future events reveal fulfillment of God's promise of glory.

But indeed, as I live, all the earth will be filled with the glory of the Lord (Numbers 14:21).

The near horizon of these days of harvest reveals God's glory rising upon the Church. The issue is His glory! The goal, the rewards, and the process, all come from the glory of the Lord.

That is what the present renewal is all about! The Lord is visiting His Church to renew and prepare her, to fashion vessels of glory who will take His love, mercy, and grace to those sitting in darkness; to come with the light of the gospel of the glory of Christ (see 2 Cor. 4:4).

*Arise, shine; for your light has come, **and the glory of the Lord has risen upon you**. For behold, darkness will cover the earth, and deep darkness the peoples; but the Lord will rise upon you, and **His glory will appear upon you**. And nations will come to your light, and kings to the brightness of your rising* (Isaiah 60:1-3).

This chapter examines the glory that comes from a greater presence of the Lord in the Church, from a deeper incarnation of God in His people. The word *"glory"* denotes the awesome, majestic splendor of His presence, words, nature, or deeds in whatever way God chooses to reveal Himself. How do we prepare for the glory that lies ahead? How does the bride make herself ready? How does she prepare for the day when He presents her to Himself in all her glory (see Eph. 5:25-27)? And finally, how can we measure our preparation? These are questions we will seek to address.

Growing Into Christ

Several years ago, while driving to fulfill a speaking engagement, I began praying for a way to teach believers how to measure their spiritual growth. The Lord spoke to my spirit and asked me how I measured my growth when I went from childhood to being an adult. Immediately, I recalled how I used to go into the bedroom at home and look at myself in the mirror. I began doing so when I was barely able to peer over the bureau on which the mirror was mounted. In this way, I watched my height increase, my biceps grow, etc., over the years.

The Lord spoke to me and said, "I also have a mirror to show how you grow in My Spirit." He then asked me how else I had monitored my growth into adulthood. As I pondered this question, I recalled how my parents' expectations of me changed as I grew up. At age six most of their concern dealt with my cleanliness, table manners, what I ate, how much sleep I needed, etc. However, when I entered my teen years, they expected me to study hard at school, do my homework, be responsible for tasks around the house, have a proper behavior socially and be concerned for my future. The Lord spoke to me and said, "I have expectations for My children too, which will also change as they grow in Me."

As I began to formulate teaching on spiritual growth using these guidelines, the Lord revealed six key words to me that described the mirror and His expectations. This is what I wish to share with you.

Since the meaning is often lost in translation, the words in question are shown in their Greek form. The meaning of these words are interpreted in the context of sentences in which they appear, so that their meaning becomes clear in English.

The Mirror

Five words comprise the mirror by revealing five distinct levels of spiritual stature from birth to maturity. These words, along with pertinent Scriptures where they appear, are shown on the following chart.

Spiritual growth cannot begin apart from a spiritual birth. Thus, the first level is defined by the word *brephos* meaning a "newborn babe."

Like newborn babes [brephos]), long for the pure milk of the word, that by it you may grow in respect to salvation (1 Peter 2:2).

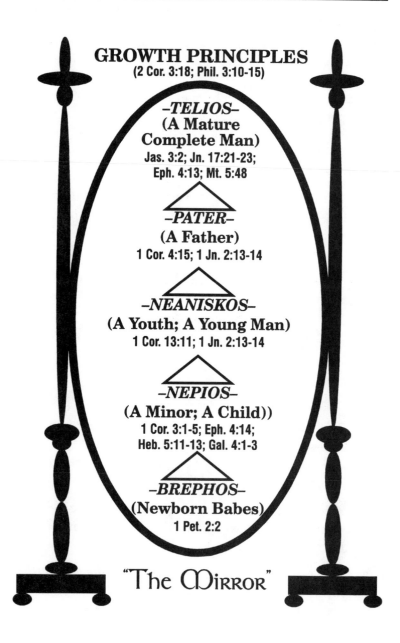

GROWTH PRINCIPLES
(2 Cor. 3:18; Phil. 3:10-15)

–TELIOS–
(A Mature
Complete Man)
Jas. 3:2; Jn. 17:21-23;
Eph. 4:13; Mt. 5:48

–PATER–
(A Father)
1 Cor. 4:15; 1 Jn. 2:13-14

–NEANISKOS–
(A Youth; A Young Man)
1 Cor. 13:11; 1 Jn. 2:13-14

–NEPIOS–
(A Minor; A Child))
1 Cor. 3:1-5; Eph. 4:14;
Heb. 5:11-13; Gal. 4:1-3

–BREPHOS–
(Newborn Babes)
1 Pet. 2:2

"The Mirror"

The primary factor related to growth at this beginning level is one's hunger for God's Word. It is a major, determining criterion for all subsequent growth, for the Lord reveals Himself and His ways through His Word. It is an appropriate question to ask ourselves every time we look into the mirror, "Do I have a hunger for the Word of God?" There will not be growth without continual feeding upon the nourishing Word of God.

The Greek word on the chart immediately above *brephos* is *nepios*, which identifies the next level of spiritual stature. Various translations of this word are "a child without words," "a minor," "a spiritually immature person," and "a babe." The significance of this word, in the sense of spiritual growth, can be seen in the context of the following verses where it is used:

> *And I, brethren, could not speak to you as to spiritual men, but as to men of flesh, as to **babes** [nepios] in Christ. I gave you milk to drink, not solid food; for you were not yet able to receive it—For since there is **jealousy** and **strife among you**, are you not fleshly, and are you not walking like mere men? For when one says, "**I am of Paul**," and another, "**I am of Apollos**," are you not mere men?* (1 Corinthians 3:1-4).

> *As a result* [i.e., of growing up] *we are no longer to be **children** [nepios], **tossed here and there by waves**, and **carried about by every wind of doctrine**, by the trickery of men, by craftiness in deceitful scheming* (Ephesians 4:14).

> *Now I say, as long as the heir is a **child** [nepios], he does not differ at all from a slave although he is owner of everything, but he is under guardians and managers until the date set by the father. So also we, while we were*

children [nepios], *were held in bondage under the elemental things of the world* (Galatians 4:1-3).

Verses 4 through 19, of the fourth chapter of Paul's epistle to the Galatian Christians, made it clear that if they fell back into legalism they would be reverting back to a *nepios* level of stature. Maturity could *only* be realized if they walked according to the law of the Spirit of life in Christ Jesus (see Rom. 8:1-4).

Concerning Him (i.e., Jesus) *we have much to say, and it is hard to explain, since you have become dull of hearing. For though by this time you ought to be teachers, you have need again for someone to teach you the elementary principles of the oracles of God, and you have* **come to need milk and not solid food**. *For* **everyone who partakes only of milk is not accustomed to the word of righteousness,** *for he is a babe* [nepios] (Hebrews 5:11-13).

One would not expect to find a believer exhibiting all the character traits of a *nepios*, but all new believers will manifest one or more of them to some degree. This is inevitable, for they reflect our fallen human nature. They are marks of one's second (spiritual) childhood; something we must all go through if we are to grow up into Christ. It is not the behavior of a *nepios* that is the problem; the problem exists when one *remains* in that state without changing. The characteristics of a *nepios* are simply manifestations of the human nature that have not yet experienced the cross of Christ. By faith, they should begin to disappear at water baptism.

Our physical bodies and minds grow naturally and mature with time. A six-year-old becomes a ten-year-old in four years. In the world of the Spirit, this is not true. Some believers will grow very quickly; while others may spend their entire lifetime without growing beyond the level of a *nepios*. One who faithfully continues to examine his life in the light of these Scriptures will see these behavioral traits less and less as he grows in Christ.

In summary, the following behavioral traits mark a *nepios* level of spiritual childhood:

✤ Jealousy, strife, and envy.

✤ Cliques; following some believer more than Christ.

✤ Continually tossed about by problems, issues, and circumstances, whether secular or spiritual.

✤ "Up" today, and "down" tomorrow.

✤ Tendency to run after new doctrines.

✤ Susceptible to cultic overtures, advertising, or the charisma of a spokesman.

✤ Legalistic lifestyle and emphasis.

✤ Continual need for re-instruction on basic doctrines; unable to instruct others in this area. Such persons would not be faithful in basic things, such as prayer, tithes, service, etc.

✤ Poor insight and little development of spiritual judgment.

There is one more observation to be made concerning a *nepios*. When the 70 disciples were sent out by Jesus to preach the gospel of the kingdom, they returned with joy and reported that even demons were subject to them in His name. In prayer to His Father, Jesus said:

> *...I praise Thee, O Father, Lord of heaven and earth, that Thou didst hide these things from the wise and intelligent and didst reveal them to **babes** [nepios]...* (Luke 10:21).

The point is, even a *nepios* has power and authority over demons. Greater is He who is in us, than he who is in the world, which is true for every child of God!

I expect some readers will question why pride was not listed as a heading characteristic of a *nepios*. The answer is that pride is behind *each* and *every nepios* trait. Pride *must* be dealt with in order to grow in Christ. When believers will not humble themselves in repentance and honestly see themselves as the Lord describes them in His word, they will remain a *nepios*.

Transition to the next level beyond *nepios* is expressed by the following scripture:

> *When I was a **child** [nepios], I used to **speak** as a **child** [nepios], **think** as a **child** [nepios] **reason** as a **child** [nepios]; when I became a man, I did away with childish things* [i.e., traits of a nepios] (1 Corinthians 13:11).

This particular level of spiritual growth is represented by the word *neaniskos,* which means "a young man." Its use in scripture suggests a victorious warrior in the prime of life, one who has defeated his enemy.

> *...I have written to you, **young men** [neaniskos], because you are **strong**, and **the word of God abides** in you, and you **have overcome the evil one*** (1 John 2:14).

This verse speaks of more than casting out demons; it points to one strong in the Spirit who is well established in the Word of God. It is one who has recognized that his mind is the *primary* battleground with satan, and has dealt with those areas of weakness that could become footholds or fortresses of influence for the enemy to attack him. He has achieved victory over such things as fantasies, unforgiveness, racism, pride, prejudices, etc. The thought patterns that mark how a *nepios thinks, reasons* and *speaks* are where the weapons of the Spirit must be applied to bring forth transition to a *neaniskos*. This only comes through practice.

> *For the weapons of our warfare are not of the flesh, but divinely powerful for the destruction of fortresses. We are destroying* **speculations** *and every* **lofty thing raised up against the knowledge of God**, *and we are taking every thought captive to the obedience of Christ* (2 Corinthians 10:4-5).

The spiritual stature of a *neaniskos* is the standard for those who God is renewing and preparing for His army in the closing days of this age.

Paters is the word marking the next measure of growth into Christ. The word means "fathers." Whatever the Lord has revealed or imparted to us by the anointing of His Spirit is never for us alone; once we have become established in new dimensions of His life, we are expected to build into others what the Lord has built into us. This can involve leading the unsaved to Christ, as Paul did the Corinthian believers, or discipling a convert toward maturity as a son, such as Paul's discipling of Timothy (see 1 Cor. 4:15; 2 Tim. 2:1-2). *Paters* is not a title or an official position; it is ministry based on relationship. This is an essential aspect of equipping others in Christ.

It might appear that once one had attained this level, he has reached maturity. Such is not the case! One of the most important characteristic of any Christian who is growing into Christ, is an ever greater realization that he (or she) has not yet arrived, nor attained the completion of that to which they have been called. The reason for this is quite simple; the more intimately we know Him and His ways, the more clearly we see how far short we are in comparison to Him. One's humility and appreciation of this difference will always increase as they grow in the Spirit. Thus, there is an attitude of mind that we must have if we are to continue to make true progress. Paul expressed it well:

> *Not that I have already obtained it, or have already become perfect, but* **I press on in order that I may lay hold of that for which also I was laid hold of by Christ Jesus**. *Brethren,* **I do not regard myself as having laid hold of it yet**; *but one thing I do: forgetting what lies behind and reaching forward to what lies ahead,* **I press on toward the goal for the upward call of God in Christ Jesus**. *Let us therefore, as many as are perfect* [i.e., mature, complete] *have this attitude...* (Philippians 3:12-15).

The final level, the goal that we have all been called to, is expressed by the word *teleios,* which means "having reached its end, to complete, to mature, to perfect." The context of the verses in which this word appears expresses the thought of having attained to all that God's grace was extended to us, either to be or to do.

> *But solid food is for the* **mature** [telios] *who because of practice have their* **senses trained to discern good and evil** (Hebrews 5:14).

> *For we all stumble in many ways. If anyone does not stumble* **in what he says,** *he is a* **perfect** [teleios] *man, able to bridle the whole body as well* (James 3:2).

However, we cannot truly mature in Christ apart from our relationship to others. The Lord seeks the corporate maturity of His body, the mature purity and love of His bride.

> *Until we all* [i.e., the entire body] *attain to the unity of the faith, and of the knowledge of the Son of God to a*

> ***mature*** [telios] *man, to the measure of the stature which belongs to the fulness* [i.e., fulfillment] *of Christ* (Ephesians 4:13).

> *I in them, and Thou in Me, that they may be **perfected** [teleios] in unity, that the world may know that Thou didst send Me, and didst love them, even as Thou didst love Me* (John 17:23).

The goal of the Lord is not individual, "perfected" disciples, but a "perfected" body, with Himself as Head. He is seeking a corporate completeness in His people. This state is described in Scripture as His bride, His body, and also as His house. The latter speaks of our relationship with one another. We are shaped, fitted, and bonded together to become the dwelling place of God in the Spirit (see Eph. 2:19-22).

> *You also, as living stones, are being built up as a spiritual house...* (1 Peter 2:5).

The following graphic illustrations show what takes place as converts to Christ are built together by fellowship and relationship into local expressions of the body of Christ. The following verbs, when combined with the words "one another," express the relational dynamics by which members are bonded together in Christ: be devoted to (one another); be kind to; be honest with; encourage; bear with; forgive; pray for; confess to; serve; care for; be patient with; show preference to; comfort; admonish; honor; bless and build up. These are ingredients of the divine cement that bonds believers together in relationship, qualities that are best developed in small group environments, such as house churches.

Difficult times are ahead; glory on the Church and darkness in the world! The Lord is moving in renewal power to prepare His people for affliction, persecution, and even martyrdom. Enduring such things will drive our roots deeper into Him.

Living Stones at the Start • Conversion

*And let endurance have its perfect result, that you may be **perfect** [teleios] and complete, lacking in nothing* (James 1:4).

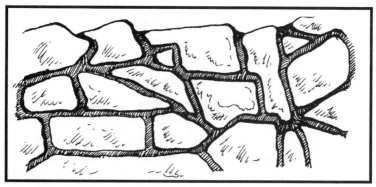

Living Stones When Relationship Has Been Built

One thing is essential for progress at each level of our growth, that is to keep our eyes on Him, beholding His glory (see 2 Cor. 3:18). This is our goal in spiritual adulthood.

These five words complete the "mirror"; let us now examine the word which expresses our Father's expectations for us.

Our Father's Expectations

The sixth Greek word is *huios,* which means "son." All born-again believers are God's sons; and He has the same supremely important goal for each one: to become conformed to the image of the Lord Jesus Christ.

Our progress toward this goal is by four progressive steps which express our Father's expectations of us as His sons. These levels are shown in the following chart along with associated Scriptures.

First, sonship begins with the new birth. We can only become spiritual sons through a spiritual birth. We will never be more of a son than we are at this time. However, as we grow up, new things will be expected of us.

*For you are all **sons** [huios] of God through faith in Christ Jesus* (Galatians 3:26).

After a time of being nourished from the milk of His Word, God begins to exercise a regimen of discipline in the lives of His sons. Discipline serves to develop obedience to His will and purpose. As we respond to Him, we will become more apparent as sons since we begin to exhibit more of the nature and purpose of our Father and less of going our own way.

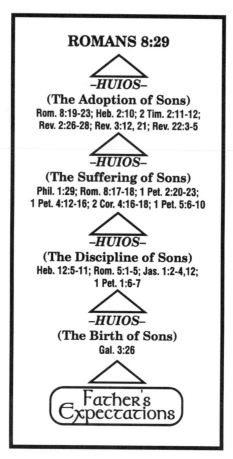

ROMANS 8:29

−HUIOS−
(The Adoption of Sons)
Rom. 8:19-23; Heb. 2:10; 2 Tim. 2:11-12;
Rev. 2:26-28; Rev. 3:12, 21; Rev. 22:3-5

−HUIOS−
(The Suffering of Sons)
Phil. 1:29; Rom. 8:17-18; 1 Pet. 2:20-23;
1 Pet. 4:12-16; 2 Cor. 4:16-18; 1 Pet. 5:6-10

−HUIOS−
(The Discipline of Sons)
Heb. 12:5-11; Rom. 5:1-5; Jas. 1:2-4,12;
1 Pet. 1:6-7

−HUIOS−
(The Birth of Sons)
Gal. 3:26

Father's Expectations

God's discipline can take many forms: teaching, corrective input from leaders, counsel and admonition from other believers, circumstances, problems, and difficult relationships. These things point out weaknesses and character flaws that perhaps we were not even aware of. Lack of humility is a common discovery. The issue is, we are expected to change, and our Father brings things into our life to effect this change.

*...My son, do not regard lightly the discipline of the Lord, nor faint when you are reproved by Him; for those whom the Lord **loves** He disciplines, and He scourges every son whom He receives. It is for discipline that you endure; God deals with you as with sons; for what son is there whom his father does not discipline? But if you are without discipline, of which all have become partakers, then you are illegitimate children and not sons. Furthermore, we had earthly fathers to discipline us, and we respected them; shall we not much rather be subject to the Father of spirits, and live? For they disciplined us for a short time as seemed best to them, but He disciplines us **for our good, that we may share His holiness**. All discipline for the moment seems not to be joyful, but sorrowful; yet to those who have been trained by it, afterwards it yields the peaceful fruit of righteousness* (Hebrews 12:5-11).

God's discipline is a distinct mark of sonship; furthermore, it never comes to an end in this life. It is something we will experience, and hopefully do so joyfully, until we go to be with Him. The Lord's dealings will vary with each one; for only He knows what He has called us to be and do, and what is lacking in each life. We must *never compare* our portion of discipline with that of other believers; to do so would be to make God appear unfair or partial. We have all observed examples of extreme hardship, persecution, trials, or calamities that others have experienced, and we have marveled how their testimonies of victory glorified the Lord. He will not allow us to be tempted beyond our ability to stand, and He will *always* provide grace to walk through the time of difficulty we face. We need to remember that He is not testing some strategy, or the devil, or the world. It is we who are being tested. If we fail the first time, there will surely come a second time, and a third time, etc. The Lord is patient with us, for

141

He is determined to strip away all confidence we have in our human strength, until we rely *only* upon Him.

An alternative word for "discipline" is "pruning."

> *I am the true vine, and My Father is the vinedresser. Every branch in Me that does not bear fruit, He takes away; and every branch that bears fruit, He prunes it, that it may bear more fruit* (John 15:1-2).

Our Father's expectation for us as His sons is to embrace His discipline to bear more fruit, becoming bondservants committed to His purpose for our generation. In this way, we prepare for a future inheritance in glory that we will share as heirs with Jesus for all eternity. This will not come to pass through any measure of human strategy or strength, but as we yield ourselves to Him, the Holy Spirit performs the work. As He does so, we will more clearly recognize our relationship as sons, and give ourselves to doing the works of a son: to destroy the forces of wickedness, to minister to the poor and needy, and to serve and care for God's heritage in His people. His glory will begin to be seen in our lives.

> *And we know that God causes **all** things to work together for **good** to those who love God, to those who are **called according to His purpose**. For whom He foreknew, He also **predestined to become conformed to the image of His Son**, that He might be the first-born among many brethren* (Romans 8:28-29).

> *In this you greatly rejoice, even though now for a little while, **if necessary**, you have been distressed by various trials, that the proof of your faith, being more precious than gold which is perishable, even though tested by fire, may be found to result in praise and glory and honor at the revelation of Jesus Christ* (1 Peter 1:6-7).

The third expectation for His sons concerns "suffering." One who has not submitted to the Father's discipline in his life will not embrace suffering; he will run from it.

> *For to you it has been granted for Christ's sake, not only to believe in Him, but also to suffer for His sake* (Philippians 1:29).

> *For you have been called for this purpose, since Christ also suffered for you, leaving you an example for you to follow in His steps* (1 Peter 2:21).

> *And if children, heirs also, heirs of God and fellow heirs with Christ,* **if indeed we suffer with Him in order that we may also be glorified with Him**. *For I consider that the* **sufferings of this present time are not worthy to be compared with the glory that is to be revealed** *to* [**in**] *us* (Romans 8:17-18).

> *But to the degree that you* **share the sufferings of Christ***, keep on rejoicing; so that also at the revelation of His glory, you may rejoice with exultation. If you are reviled for the name of Christ, you are blessed, because the* **Spirit of glory and of God rests upon you** (1 Peter 4:13-14).

> *And* **after you have suffered** *for a little while, the God of all grace, who called you to His eternal glory in Christ,* **will Himself perfect, confirm, strengthen and establish you** (1 Peter 5:10).

No one looks forward to the possibility of having to suffer. As it has in past generations, martyrdom will almost certainly be a gateway to glory for some. While a crown of glory need not require physical death, it does require laying down our soul-life to do His will. The difficult experiences and trials we encounter cause us to turn to Him for wisdom and strength. Problems are simply opportunities to mature in faithfulness and perseverance.

The ease and comforts of this world, and a spirit of lethargy will hinder and frustrate the process of preparing for the glory to come. Glory comes out of the harness of God's discipline, affliction, persecution, and suffering. And it will involve pain!

> *For momentary, light affliction is producing for us an eternal weight of glory far beyond all comparison* (2 Corinthians 4:17).

The fourth and final level expressing God's expectation for His sons is "adoption," which concerns our place in His eternal kingdom. The word "adoption" comes from the Greek word *huiothes* which means "to place as a son." It has nothing to do with placing a son into a family by birth, or by legal adoption as in our western culture. It is based on Hebrew custom, in which newborn sons were kept under the supervision of servants until around 12 years of age. At that time, they were formally "placed as sons," that is, they were put in position as sons so that the dignity of their father-son relationship would be recognized by all. From that point in time, they assumed a growing share in the responsibilities that their father intended for them.

> *In love He **predestined us to adoption as sons through Christ Jesus to Himself,** according to the kind intention of His will, to the praise of the glory of His grace, which He freely bestowed on us in the Beloved* (Ephesians 1:4-6).

Today, we experience the spirit of adoption; in the future we will enter adoption in full, something that cannot take place until we receive bodies of glory at the resurrection.

> *For I consider the sufferings of this present time are* **not worthy to be compared with the glory** *that is to be revealed to us. For the anxious longing of the creation waits eagerly for the revealing of the sons of God. For the creation was subjected to futility* [i.e., emptiness, worthlessness] *not of its own will, but because of Him who subjected it, in hope that the creation itself also will be set free from its slavery to corruption into the freedom of the glory of the children of God. For we know that the whole creation groans and suffers the pains of childbirth together until now. And not only this, but also we ourselves having the first fruits of the Spirit, even we ourselves groan within ourselves waiting eagerly for our adoption as sons,* **the redemption of our body** (Romans 8:18-23).

The discipline we go through, the trials, afflictions and suffering that we endure in our service to Him, how well we obey Him and represent His heart to others, together determine how we will be placed as sons in the future. Our Father expects us to go through these things so that we will become more like Jesus. There will be distinct differences in glory that believers have in the age to come. And this glory will reflect the authority and responsibility that each son is given as they are placed in realms of oversight.

> *...for if we died with Him, we shall also live with Him; if we endure, we shall also reign with Him...* (2 Timothy 2:11-12).

At that time, His sons will be unveiled to all of creation in their glorified bodies; sons who have prepared themselves to rule with Christ in glory from the city of His eternal rest. This placing of His sons is the completion of their adoption; it is the final expectation of our Father in Heaven for His sons (see Dan. 7:18,22,27).

God's expectation for His children is glory! His wisdom, a mystery hidden since the ages began, was predestined to prepare us as vessels for glory; to rule and reign with the Lord of glory.

> *For it was fitting for Him, for whom are all things, and through whom are all things, in bringing many sons to glory...* (Hebrews 2:10).

This is what our Father expects of us!

Finally, whether we are looking into His mirror or considering His expectations for us, we must *never* compare ourselves, our stature, or our cross with other Christians. One can only understand his true stature and growth by keeping his eyes fixed on Jesus. This will *guarantee* humility to all who do so honestly!

There *never* should be a time when we cannot see ourselves as *little children sitting at the feet of our Father,* and growing in the grace and knowledge of our Lord and Savior, Jesus Christ—childlike, but not childish.

The significance of glory becomes more apparent when we examine the difference between our inheritance and our rewards in Christ.

Our Inheritance

When parents die and bequeath an estate to their offspring, the inheritance is given to the children simply because it was promised to them in the will of their parents. They did *not* merit it nor earn it; it became theirs by *promise*, and promise alone.

In the same way, our inheritance in Christ is based on what God has promised in His Word. These promises become ours, when by His grace, we truly repent and through faith accept Jesus Christ as Savior and Lord. Our inheritance includes *all* of the blessings of eternal life, which can never be earned or merited by race, culture, or good deeds; they are entirely a free gift from God!

> *For this reason it is by **faith**, that it might be in accordance **with grace**, in order that the promise may be certain to all the descendants, not only to those who are of the Law, but also to those who are of the faith of Abraham, who is the father of us all* (Romans 4:16).

Thus, our inheritance, which accompanies the salvation of our soul, is by grace on the basis of our faith in the promises of the gospel; we are heirs according to promise (see Gal. 3:29). As believers, we must never consider ourselves unworthy of this great inheritance. Of course, we are unworthy, but Christ has made us worthy, for He has paid the price for all of it!

The following seven promises define our inheritance:

1. Eternal Life
   And this is the promise which He himself made to us: eternal life (1 John 2:25).

   Eternal life, which begins with the new birth, is to know God and to forever live in fellowship with Him (see 1 Jn. 5:10-13).

2. To Be Indwelt by the Holy Spirit
   *In order that in Christ Jesus the blessing of Abraham might come to the Gentiles, so that **we might receive the promise of the Spirit** through faith* (Galatians 3:14).

   *For the **promise** [of the Holy Spirit] is for you and your children, and for all who are afar off, as many as the Lord our God shall call* (Acts 2:39).

No one can be a child of God apart from the convicting work of the Holy Spirit. We cannot know the promptings of God apart from the leading of His Spirit. Our inheritance also includes all the virtues and power of the Spirit. And He is the Spirit who will lead us into all truth. He is our anointing to break the chains of those who are bound by satan. He sanctifies us, reveals Christ to us, and teaches us how to worship and pray.

3. The Family of God
   Whoever receives the life and nature of God through the new birth becomes a son. He is their Father and each one has the place and esteem of a son in His household (see 1 Jn. 3:1-2).

   If we were to visit an earthly family with many sons we would likely find one in diapers, several in various levels of childhood, and possibly, one or more older ones who were helping their parents with various household responsibilities. All children would be loved equally, but their responsibilities would be quite different. It is similar in God's family. Each of us are special in the eyes of our Father. There are *no* second-class citizens in His household; all sons share His love equally.

4. The Body of Christ
   To be a son of God, to belong to Christ, is to also be a member of His body, the Church. This is our inheritance in Him. The body of Christ is made up of *all* who are called out of the world into fellowship with one another to make up one Church. The word "church" is translated from a Greek word, *ekklesia,* which is composed of two words that mean "to call" and "from out of." There may be many religious organizations and denominations, but there is only one Church.

5. The Kingdom of God
   To belong to God is to be a citizen of His kingdom. This is our inheritance in Christ.

   For He delivered us from the domain of darkness, and transferred us to the kingdom of His beloved Son, in whom we have redemption, the forgiveness of sins (Colossians 1:13-14).

   Our inheritance includes victory over all the schemes of satan and his kingdom of darkness. There is a future, much greater dimension of God's kingdom that will one day include all of the earth as well as Heaven. This is also the inheritance of all saints (see Dan. 7:18,27). It will be ruled by the Lord Jesus Christ, with each saint having a specific place of service.

6. Resurrection
   Flesh and blood cannot inherit the kingdom of God. For this reason, every believer is promised a resurrection of life. The promise that we will be resurrected to live forever was made by Jesus Himself.

   Jesus said to her, "I am the resurrection and the life; he who believes in Me shall live even if he dies, and everyone who lives and believes in Me shall never die..." (John 11:25-26).

   We receive our new bodies when the Lord Jesus returns in glory at the last trumpet to raise from the dead all who belong to Him.

   Behold, I tell you a mystery; we shall not all sleep, but we shall all be changed, in a moment, in the twinkling of an eye, at the last trumpet; for the trumpet will sound, and the dead will be raised imperishable, and we shall be changed (1 Corinthians 15:51-52).

7. The Image of Jesus

Resurrection is the miracle of putting off our earthly house of clay, and putting on the house prepared for us in Heaven (see 2 Cor. 5:1-5). We replace a body of death with a spiritual body that is imperishable. This is the inheritance of every believer.

And just as we have borne the image of the earthly, we shall also bear the image of the heavenly (1 Corinthians 15:49).

What will our glorified body be like? We are promised that we will inherit a body which reflects the image of Jesus. This does not mean that we would have the same glory He does, or even the same glory as other believers.

*Beloved, now we are children of God, and it has not appeared as yet what we shall be. We know that, when He appears, **we shall be like Him**, because we shall see Him just as He is* (1 John 3:2).

The desire of our Father's heart is to have many sons who manifest the image of His only begotten Son. This has been His purpose from the beginning of creation.

These seven magnificent promises, all based on the grace of God, make up the inheritance of *every* person who becomes a child of God. That part of our inheritance, which we have yet to receive, is reserved for us in heaven.

*To obtain an inheritance which is **imperishable** and undefiled and will not fade away, reserved in heaven for you* (1 Peter 1:4).

The only place for boasting in regard to our inheritance is in the person and sacrifice of Christ.

Let us now consider how the Lord will reward His followers in the resurrection.

Our Rewards

*For we must **all** appear before the judgment seat of Christ, that **each one** may be recompensed for his deeds in the body, according to **what he has done**, whether good or bad* (2 Corinthians 5:10).

Rewards will be based on God's assessment of our stewardship of the inheritance we received in Christ (i.e., how well we obeyed Him with all that He bequeathed to us at Calvary). Although we may be conscious only of great personal needs when coming to Christ, once we are born again we discover something new. We are no longer our own! We have been bought with a price (see 1 Cor. 6:19-20). We discover that we have been saved to serve in a purpose which God has been bringing to pass over the centuries. Each of us has been called in our generation to a unique and specific place of service in the body of Christ.

No one will be coerced, for service must come out of willing, submitted hearts, and we will be judged according to the following four principles:

✤ The quality of what we do will depend on the extent that Christ is Lord in our life.

✤ The only valid service is that accomplished by the anointing of the Holy Spirit. The arm of flesh cannot do the works of God.

✤ While inheritance is entirely based on grace, service requires our commitment and obedience in *working with the grace* of God that is extended to us according

151

to our personal call (see Rom. 12:6). Paul expressed it well:

But by the grace of God I am what I am, and His grace toward me did not prove vain; but I labored even more than all of them [the other apostles], *yet not I, **but the grace of God with me*** (1 Corinthians 15:10).

❖ We are not called to serve alone. Our specific gifting for service should take place in a local body where we are committed, accountable, and supported by other members. How well we relate to other members will also determine the quality of our service.

Since each believer begins as a newborn babe in Christ, it is only possible to walk and serve in these principles by growing in spiritual stature. The quality of our service, and thus our rewards, will be reflected by our spiritual growth in Christ. In God's plan for each of His children there is more concern for their maturity in Him than in how well they perform.

It is apparent that while all believers are equal in their inheritance, this is not the case for rewards. Each person will be honored according to his works, and there will be degrees of "greatness" in this respect; Jesus speaks of "the least," "the great" and "the greatest" in His kingdom (see Lk. 7:28; Mt. 5:19; 18:4). One would not expect the prophet Jonah to receive the same reward as Isaiah, Jeremiah, or Daniel.

*Now he who plants and he who waters are one; but each will receive his own reward **according to his own labor*** (1 Corinthians 3:8).

Some saints bear fruit a hundredfold, some sixty- and some thirtyfold. That is the principle of rewards!

The Reward of Glory

There is a remarkable verse in the Epistle to Hebrews.

*Women received back their dead by resurrection; and others were tortured, not accepting their release, in order that they might obtain **a better resurrection*** (Hebrews 11:35).

Because these individuals were children of God, they were assured of a resurrection to life. What did the writer mean, "to obtain a better resurrection"? Scripture appears to suggest that "glory" is what marks a better resurrection.

*There is one glory of the sun, and another glory of the moon, and another glory of the stars; for star differs from star in glory. **So also is the resurrection of the dead**. It is sown a perishable body...**it is raised in glory**...* (1 Corinthians 15:41-43).

Before they sinned, our first parents were apparently clothed in glory. It was after their sin that they discovered they were naked. Their covering of glory was gone. It is one thing to be saved and go to Heaven; it is quite another to be clothed with the glory of Christ. We do need to be concerned about the glory of our resurrected body. Every believer will have his works tested by the fire of God (see 1 Cor. 3:10-15). A Christian's service of wood, hay, and straw will be burned up. Having one's works burned up speaks of nakedness.

*For indeed in this house we groan, longing to be clothed with our dwelling from heaven; inasmuch as we, **having put it on, shall not be found naked*** (2 Corinthians 5:2-3).

The ultimate reward set before us by our Lord is to gain His glory. Nothing can be greater than this! God desires to remove the veil of religion from His people so that they can behold His glory.

> *...because God has chosen you from the beginning for salvation through sanctification by the Spirit and faith in the truth. And it was for this He called you through our gospel, that **you might gain the glory of our Lord Jesus Christ** (2 Thessalonians 2:13-14).*

This points to where our hope is to be fixed, for glory reflects the purpose of God which He has planned from the beginning for us.

> *Through whom also we have obtained our introduction by faith into this grace in which we stand; and **we exult in hope of the glory of God** (Romans 5:2).*

> *But we all, as with unveiled face, we see as in a mirror the Lord's glory reflected, are changed into the same likeness **from one degree of glory to another**, derived as it is from the Lord, who is the Spirit (2 Corinthians 3:18 Berkeley).*

The Lord used the following parables in His teaching to clearly set forth the principles upon which rewards will be based:

❖ The slaves who were rewarded or punished according to their stewardship while their master was absent from them (see Lk. 12:42-48).

❖ The parable of the talents (see Mt. 25:14-30; Lk. 19:13-26).

❖ The parable of the ten virgins (see Mt. 25:1-10).

The theme of these parables challenge us to lay hold of God's promises and set our heart fully upon Him, so that we will not lose the glory that could be ours in the age to come.

Set your mind on the things above, *not on the things that are on earth. For you have died and your life is hidden with Christ in God. When Christ, who is our life, is revealed, then you also will be revealed with Him **in glory*** (Colossians 3:2-4).

The Glory of Revival

While there may well be no pattern in Church history for the great revival that lies before us, certain spiritual principles are always required for the glory of God to be present.

In his record[23] of the "Azusa Street Revival" during the early part of this century, Frank Bartleman describes both how the Spirit of God was hindered or quenched in those days, as well as what encouraged His presence. There were three truths in particular that Bartleman emphasized in this respect:

1. A revival should not be institutionalized; men must not control what God is doing.

2. A deep burden of intercessory prayer is needed to birth what only God can accomplish.

3. The one supremely important goal and objective for believers is to know Christ! Intimacy with Him brings His glory into what takes place. Doctrines, experiences, miracles, manifestations, ministries only have significance to the extent that Christ is preached and glorified. When this truth is weak, wrong emphasis and exaggerations begin to appear and the glory of God's presence lifts.[24]

These are good words of advice for the Church in this day of visitation.

155

The Glory of Thankfulness

A heart attitude that marked Israel's failures was their frequent grumblings (see 1 Cor. 10:10). The same attitude will be in those whom the Lord judges in the day of His wrath (see Jude 14-16). Lack of thankfulness is the seed of grumbling, and this is a weakness in the Church of America today, as is a lack of awe for God.

Just as grumbling and complaining mark the disobedient, so thankfulness is a sign of divine sonship (see Phil. 2:14-15).

Thankfulness is a fruit of humility, and is cultivated through worship. It is the essence of how to come into His presence.

Enter His gates with thanksgiving, and His courts with praise. Give thanks to Him; bless His name (Psalm 100:4).

The release of God's power through His people comes through prayer and worship. Worship is the universal language of spiritual warfare. The power of satan cannot stand before it. Worship is essentially three expressions of the human heart: rejoicing or joy, prayer, and thanksgiving (see 1 Thess. 5:16-18; Phil. 4:4-7). We are to never take God for granted, but to come before Him in reverential awe with thanksgiving. If we possess Him, we possess all things. Thanks be to God for His indescribable gift!

Glory of the Bride

As the purpose of God unfolds for His people, the Church will be seen in three different ways.

1. From satan's point of view, she will be a mighty army waging war against him under the leadership of the Lord Jesus.

2. For those who turn to the Lord from the deep darkness enveloping the world, she will be a refuge, a place of salvation, a spiritual hospital.

3. From the Lord's viewpoint, she will be His bride who has prepared herself for His return; a bride in army boots!

When one considers the glory of the bride of Christ, a question arises, "Is the bride a separate group who is uniquely distinct from the Church; or is she an integral part of the Church?" The following are reasons why the latter is a correct view.

Scripture is emphatic that, in God's eyes, the Church is the one all inclusive body of believers united in Christ (see Jn. 17:21-23). The Lord has promised that, although individual rewards may vary greatly, the whole Church will be presented holy and blameless to Him. The glory of His presence will clothe her. This glory will not be based on how much we love God, but on how much He loves us; not our commitment to Him but His commitment to us.

In a great mansion, there are vessels with a special place of honor because of their distinctive utility and beauty, being made of gold, silver, or precious jewels. There are also many commonplace vessels made of inexpensive material such as earthenware, which have much less honor. This is analogous to how believers in the resurrection will make up the dwelling place that God is building today for the place of His eternal rest. It is in this sense that the following statement is true, "The garments we are weaving today are the ones we will wear for all eternity." Now is the time to establish the reward and glory of our resurrection.

Spiritual pride, elitism, and sectarianism inevitably will arise whenever a body of believers see and proclaim themselves as a special group with a "higher rating" in God's eyes than the rest of Christendom. This can arise from doctrine, religious practices, or from allegiance to a charismatic leader who claims to have special revelation and authority from God. Such groups bring division to the body of Christ and are a sign of immaturity.

There is no doubt that there will be "special distinctions" in the resurrection. However, these must come from the Lord Himself when He rewards His disciples. We are *never* to presume such honor for ourselves today.

A quality of the bride is her obedience in deeds of righteousness.

> *Let us rejoice and be glad and give the glory to Him, for the marriage of the Lamb has come and **His bride has made herself ready**. And it was given to her to clothe herself in fine linen, bright and clean; for the fine linen is the **righteous acts** of the saints* (Revelation 19:7-8).

Another quality of the bride is that she represents the city which God has been preparing over the centuries for His final dwelling place, the glory of His presence, the place of His eternal rest among mankind. She will come down to earth clothed with the glory of God, uniquely prepared for His presence.

> *And I saw the **holy city**, new Jerusalem, coming down out of heaven from God, **made ready as a bride** adorned for her husband* (Revelation 21:2).

*...and showed me the holy city, Jerusalem, coming down out of heaven from God, **having the glory of God**...And the city has no need of the sun or of the moon to shine upon it, **for the glory of God has illumined it**, and its lamp is the Lamb* (Revelation 21:10,11,23).

Those who overcome in this life have specific promises concerning their place with the Lord in His eternal city, and their place of authority in the city of God.

***He who overcomes**, I will make him a pillar in the temple of My God, and **he will not go out from it anymore**; and I will write upon him the name of My God, and **the name of the city of My God, the New Jerusalem**, which comes down out of heaven from God, and My new name* (Revelation 3:12).

***He who overcomes,** I will grant to him to sit down with Me on My throne, as I also overcame and sat down with My Father on His throne* (Revelation 3:21).

*. . . and the throne of God and of the Lamb shall be in it [the city], and **His bond-servants** shall serve Him; and they shall see His face, and His name shall be on their foreheads . . . and they **shall reign forever and ever*** (Revelation 22:3-5).

*And **he who overcomes**, and **he who keeps My deeds until the end**, to him I will give authority over the nations; and he shall rule them with a rod of iron...* (Revelation 2:26-27)

Today—intimacy, preparation, and harvest; tomorrow—union and reigning with Christ; the purpose of God fulfilled!

Conclusion

I have earnestly prayed while writing this book for words to express the Lord's heart. Nothing else is really important; it is pointless to add another book to the many that already exist, unless in some measure, I speak for the Lord.

We are living in a unique period of Church history, one that is perilous with potential for spiritual deception and darkness, but also one that is pregnant with hope for the glory to be birthed in the age to come. It is wise to seek understanding of what will mark the transition from this age into the future when the whole earth will be filled with His glory.

I cannot set dates, or even be sure which generation certain prophecies will apply to. However, one thing is sure, our eyes are to be wholly on the Lord. Our emphasis should not be on what satan is doing; it should be on the purpose of God for this hour.

The following observations represent an overview of how I perceive this transition taking place in the years ahead.

❖ We are living in the beginning of a day of God's visitation. It is vital that the Church not be as Israel and fail to recognize this truth (see Mt. 16:1-3; Lk. 19:42-44). Never before in Church history has the future estate of believers been so dependent upon recognizing their day of visitation.

❖ Although currently in renewal phase, I believe this move of God will eventually result in the greatest revival of the Church. Because it is birthed by the sovereignty of God, *it must not be institutionalized;* it is intended to bless the whole body of Christ, and to impact all nations. For that reason, wisdom and godly shepherding of what takes place is essential.[25]

❖ God has a twofold purpose for the Church: to equip her to gather in the final, great end-time harvest of souls (fulfillment of the Old Testament Feast of Tabernacles); and to prepare her for His return, when He will present her to Himself in all her glory.

❖ The Church is not ready for the task ahead, and the Lord is moving in renewal power to turn the hearts of His people to Himself and His purpose for these days. He is doing a deep work in hearts, revealing how much He loves us, building new intimacy, and encouraging us to receive His love and give it away. Spiritual songs from Heaven reveal the heart and strategy of the Lord. Worship brings His presence and releases His power in the Church. He is calling His people to intercession, humility, and unity; to take His love to the streets. Through supernatural outpourings of the Holy Spirit, the Lord will reveal His great grace, love, mercy, and power to the nations through the Church. Multitudes will come to Him as the greatest force in the universe, the love of God, touches their hearts.

❖ Each believer can become a fruitful reaper to the extent he (or she) is in union with the Lord and have found his place of service as an accountable member of a local church. The Lord is going to use children in a wonderful way. All members will be required for the harvest; and unity of the body of Christ is essential.

❖ God's people will be delivered from the bondages of legalism, manipulation, and control by religious self-seeking men, and brought into the glorious freedom of His sons.

❖ The Lord will arise to shake everything that can be shaken, so that only what is of God will stand. Nations, economic structures, religious systems, and the powers of Heaven will be affected. The fire of God's judgment will touch nations calling the people to repentance.

Judgment will begin in His house, for there is great need for new wineskins that are adequate to preserve the wine of His Spirit.

❖ Transition from the present into the future is destined to take place in a time of deep darkness and spiritual deception in the world; but it will also be a time when the glory of God rests upon the church. All men will be polarized by events to choose either the way of God or the way of darkness. Great power in manifold signs and wonders will accompany preaching of the gospel. Climactic events destined by God will remove all tares from the wheat, and separate His people unto Himself. Difficulties, afflictions and persecution will be great. Daniel prophesied that in the last days many will purged, purified, and refined while none of the wicked will understand what is taking place. Those who do have insight will lead many to righteousness (see Dan. 12:3,10). Even when standing in the midst of darkness and turmoil, the glorious reality is that we are seated with Him in heavenly places. Being in union with our Lord, we enter into His rest and victory! In this way, we will partake of the glory that is to be revealed.

The Holy Spirit is moving over all the earth; the love of God is being lavishly poured out. Clouds of blessing hang low over the Church. The best wine has been kept for the end. Behold the harvest, and hear the voice of the Lord: *"Turn to Me, and be saved, all the ends of the earth..."* (Isaiah 45:22).

And the Spirit and the bride say, "Come." And let the one who hears say, "Come." And let the one who is thirsty come; let the one who wishes take the water of life without cost (Revelation 22:17).

Appendix

The Man of Lawlessness

My Objective

My objective is to address the above subject as it is described in Second Thessalonians 2:1-12. I am presenting what I believe to be a viable interpretation that is consistent with end-time events, as they are now being revealed in the closing days of this age of grace.

Revelation of the man of lawlessness is clearly presented in the first three verses as an event that must precede the coming of our Lord Jesus Christ.

Because of the unprecedented evil and deception of those days, it is vital for the Church to be well informed on this eschatological person who will be the ultimate embodiment of evil in the world, and what brings about his appearance.

Paul had previously taught the Thessalonica church on this subject; however, no record of that teaching is available to us apart from his brief reference to it in this chapter.

Since other verses are unambiguous, only verses 6 and 7 are being examined here. These two verses are translated as follows in the *New American Standard*.

And you know what restrains (him) now, so that in his time he may be revealed [vs. 6].

For the mystery of lawlessness is already at work; only he who now restrains will do so until he is taken out of the way [vs. 7].

Most Bible translators interpret these verses by assuming that satan is currently under some kind of restraint which will one day be removed. This restraining force is most often believed to be the Holy Spirit who will be removed from the scene when the church is raptured (some translators ascribe the restraining influence to other agents, such as Michael, the sovereignty of God, or civil government).

In any case, the removal of restraint will result in appearance of the man of lawlessness, also referred to as the anti-christ, the son of perdition, or a beast to whom satan, as the dragon, gives his evil nature, power, and authority (see Rev. 13). However, I believe a more likely interpretation of these verses is that satan is the one exercising the restraint, and is the one who will be revealed (in the man of lawlessness).

Verse Six

No other language can capture the fullness of what is expressed in Greek. Therefore, translators will occasionally add words in English for which there is no equivalent Greek word. They do so for one of the following three reasons:

❖ It is essential to convey the sense

❖ It is required by the context

❖ It is implied by the Greek text

These added words are generally italicized or shown in brackets. The word "him" in verse 6 is such an example. Since this word is not added in all translations, the reason for adding it appears to come from a theology that believes satan is being restrained.

For example, the following four translations, which are based on different Greek texts, do not insert "him" in verse 6.

❖ *The Interlinear Bible;* Green, (1976). Based on the Greek received text.

❖ *The Concordant Literal New Testament*; A.E. Knoch (1996). Based on Weymouth's Resultant Greek Text.

❖ *The Englishman's Greek New Testament;* Bagster (1958). Based on Stephen's Greek text, and using readings of Elizevir, Greisbach, Lachman, Gischendorf, Fregelles, Alford and Wordsworth.

❖ *The Interlinear Greek-English New Testament;* Marshall (1975).

In fact, there is nothing in the Greek text or grammar that prevents the one restraining from also being the one who is revealed. I believe this to be the case and that this person is satan.

The neuter participle in verse 6 for "what restrains" refers to the restraining influence; the masculine participle in verse 7 refers to the one doing the restraining.

The Greek verb translated as "restrain" is *katecho,* which means to "hold fast," "to detain," "hold back," or "to restrain." It is a transitive verb, so that an object must be supplied. If "hold fast" is employed as the verb, then the object would be his position in the heavenlies from which he will be ejected by Michael in spiritual warfare. This is the interpretation given by E.W. Bullinger in his footnotes on Second Thessalonians chapter 2, verse 6, in the Companion Bible.

However, if restrain (or detain) is used for the verb, the object would be the Church on earth. In my opinion, this is probably what is meant in the light of verse 7 and also Revelation chapter 12, verses 7 through 12.

Satan was totally defeated at the cross, and all that believers need for victory over him is provided by our faith in this provision. We have access directly to the throne of God and His grace for all of our needs. However, most Christians do not walk in the reality of this truth, and for this reason they are hindered by satan's accusations, spirits of condemnation, depression, etc. However, God has promised to remove this evil restraining force in the heavenlies, and bring His Church into fullness of power and authority; one upon whom His glory will arise. The phrase "in his time" makes it clear that the initiation of warfare by Michael is under God's sovereign control.

Verse Seven

The primary issue in this verse is translation of the Greek words *ginomai* and *mesos,* which are rendered "taken" and "way" in the *New American Standard.* The meaning of *Ginomai* is "to come into being," "to happen," or "to become." In the New Testament it is translated in various forms of "coming" or "coming to be" 102 times; in forms of "to become" 146 times; and in forms of "to happen," 45 times.

According to *Young's Analytical Concordance to the Bible,* *ginomai* is translated as "taken" only this once.

The Greek word *mesos* means "middle" or "in the midst." In 47 occurrences in the New Testament it is translated "way" in only two places.

The Word of God is divinely inspired, and this must begin with the Greek text. If God had intended His word to say "taken out of the way" there were far more appropriate Greek words available for use.

The theologian, George Eldon Ladd, states in his book *The Blessed Hope* (page 95) that the phrase in verse 7 "until he is taken out of the way" translates literally as "until he comes out of the midst."

Thus, it is appropriate to translate verse 7 as follows:

For the mystery of lawlessness is already at work; only he who now restrains will do so until he comes to be out of the midst.

Ginomai is a deponent verb, meaning that the verb action is not from an outside source. Satan is forced out of the heavenlies by Michael and his angels (see Rev. 12:7-9; Dan. 12:1). The subsequent action by satan after his ejection is to invest or impart his nature, power, and authority in the individual, who because of this impartation, is transformed into the man of lawlessness. This evil person is suddenly revealed in society; he comes to be or appears, out of the midst of the people living on earth. Satan thus reveals himself in and through the man of lawlessness. The verb *ginomai* denotes satan's action in achieving this revelation of himself, so that it is a deponent verb with active voice. At this time, the heavens will be open and clear from satan's presence.

Conclusion

The *Concordant Literal New Testament* translates these verses as follows:

And now you are aware what is detaining, for him to be unveiled in his own era. For the secret of lawlessness is already operating, only when the present detainer may be coming to be out of the midst, then will be unveiled the lawless one....

I believe this is an accurate translation of the verses in question. It is key in understanding that revelation of the man of lawlessness, which will occur in a time of deep darkness on earth, also means that the heavens above the Church will be free of his influence. This will provide, for the first time in Church history, a God-ordained atmosphere of relationship with His people so that God's glory will rest upon the whole Church in a final, unprecedented demonstration of His power and authority. The Lord is going to reveal a great fullness of Himself in His body, His bride! This is the significance of Revelation 12:10:

Now the salvation, and the power, and the kingdom of our God and the authority of His Christ have come, for the accuser of our brethren has been thrown down, who accuses them before our God day and night.

The Church that Jesus returns for will be a victorious Church upon whom the glory of God will rest; and this will take place as deep darkness covers the earth and the man of lawlessness is unveiled. The Lord will use the deception of that time of darkness as a deluding influence to separate tares out from among His people (see 2 Thess. 2:9-12; Mt. 13:38-41).

Endnotes

1. Clay Sterrett, *The Judgments of God* (Staunton, VA: CFC Literature, 1994).

2. Arthur Wallis, *China Miracle* (Columbia, MI: City Hill Publishing, 1986).

3. John Arnott, *The Father's Blessing* (Orlando, FL: Creation House, 1995).

4. John White, *When the Spirit Comes With Power* (Downer's Grove, IL: Intervarsity Press, 1988).

5. Rick Joyner, *The Harvest* (Charlotte, NC: Morningstar Publications).

6. Dale Rumble, *And Then the End Shall Come* (Shippensburg, PA: Destiny Image, 1991).

7. John Sieivert, John Kenyon, *Mission Handbook* (Monrovia, CA: Marc, 1993 - 95).

8. Dean Sherman, *Spiritual Warfare For Every Christian* (Seattle, WA: YWAM Publishing).

9. Donald Rumble, *Dawning Glory* (Glasco, NY: Donald Rumble, 1995).

10. Reuven Doron, *One New Man* (Cedar Rapids, IA: Reuven Doron, 1993).

11. Arthur Wallis, *China Miracle* (Columbia, MI: City Hill Publishing, 1986).

12. Michael Brown, *The End of the American Gospel Enterprise* (Shippensburg, PA: Destiny Image, 1989), p. 91.

13. Rick Joyner, *"The Quest of Kings," The Morning Star Journal* (Charlotte, NC: Morningstar Publications, 1996), Vol. 6, No. 2, p. 5.

14. James Rutz, *The Open Church* (Auburn, ME: The Seed Sowers, 1992).

15. Dale Rumble, *The Diakonate* (Shippensburg, PA: Destiny Image, 1990).

16. Dale Rumble, *Crucible of the Future* (Shippensburg, PA : Destiny Image, 1989), pp. 16-48.

17. Donald Rumble, *Apostolic and Prophetic Foundations* (Glasco, NY: Donald Rumble, 1996).

18. John Dawson, *Taking Our Cities For God* (Lake Mary, FL: Creation House, 1989).

19. James Garrett, *The Doulos Principle: Called To Be God's Slaves* (Tulsa, OK: Tulsa Christian Fellowship).

20. Francis Frangipane, *The Three Battlegrounds* (Marion, IA: Francis Frangipane, 1989).

21. Dale Rumble, *And Then the End Shall Come* (Shippensburg, PA: Destiny Image, 1991).

22. John Dawson, *Taking Our Cities For God* (Lake Mary, FL: Creation House, 1989).

23. Frank Bartleman, *Another Wave of Revival* (Springdale, PA: Whitaker House, 1982).

24. Mike Bickle, *Passion for Jesus* (Orlando, FL: Creation House, 1993).

25. Carl Kinbar, *Renewal Ministry* (Lake Katrine, NY: Fountain of Life Publications, 1995).

Other *exciting titles* by Dale Rumble

THE DIAKONATE

Rumble's book is a significant contribution to the understanding of God's people on the subject of building the Church. By carefully presenting the Bible's clear but much-neglected revelation on this subject, the author has allowed his manuscript to be lifted well above the category of "just another book" and into the very mainstream of God's great purposes in the earth.
ISBN 1-56043-020-6 $7.99p

CRUCIBLE OF THE FUTURE

Rumble, a former IBM futurist, has tremendous prophetic insight into where the Church is now and where it is headed in the decade to come. He provides a prophetic look into the 1990's and beyond.
ISBN 0-914903-89-6 $7.99p

PREPARED FOR HIS GLORY

Here is a fresh view of what God is doing in the Church. Unique illustrations are woven together with text into clear, concise expositions on how to make biblical disciples and equip believers for service, foundational truths for building "New Testament" assemblies, and end-time Church restoration.
ISBN 0-914903-08-X $9.99p

AND THEN THE END SHALL COME

What sound do anointed ears, listening to the Spirit of God, hear in this mighty hour? This former IBM futurist explores how the gospel of the Kingdom relates to the end of the age and how individual believers and the Church fit into God's great end-time strategy. This is exciting and rewarding reading!
ISBN 1-56043-063-X $8.99p

Available at your local Christian bookstore.

Internet: http://www.reapernet.com

Prices subject to change without notice.

D Destiny Image
Revival Books

IMAGES OF REVIVAL
by Richard and Kathryn Riss.

"Revival" means many things to many people. But what is real revival actually like? In this brief overview, the authors examine the many images of revivals that have occurred throughout the years. God's moves upon His people are exciting and sometimes unexpected. Learn how revival could come to your community!
ISBN 1-56043-687-5 $9.99p

FLASHPOINTS OF REVIVAL
by Geoff Waugh.

Throughout history, revival has come to various countries and peoples. Why those times? Why those people? Why not others? This book takes you inside the hearts and minds of people who lived through the major revivals of the past years. Discover how today's revivals fit into God's timeline of awakenings.
ISBN 0-7684-1002-9 $9.99p

SHARE THE FIRE
by Guy Chevreau.

Do you panic when you hear the word *evangelism*? Do you feel awkward "forcing" your opinions on another? All that changes when God abundantly and freely fills you with His Spirit! In *Share the Fire* you'll learn how God has intended evangelism to be: a bold and free work of Christ in you and through you!
ISBN 1-56043-688-3 $9.99p

THE LOST ART OF INTERCESSION
by Jim W. Goll.

How can you experience God's anointing power as a result of your own prayer? Learn what the Moravians discovered during their 100-year prayer Watch. They sent up prayers; God sent down His power. Jim Goll, who ministers worldwide through a teaching and prophetic ministry, urges us to heed Jesus' warning to "watch." Through Scripture, the Moravian example, and his own prayer life, Jim Goll proves that "what goes up must come down."
ISBN 1-56043-697-2 $9.99p

Available at your local Christian bookstore.

Internet: http://www.reapernet.com

Prices subject to change without notice.

Destiny Image
Revival Books

LET NO ONE DECEIVE YOU
by Dr. Michael L. Brown.
No one is knowingly deceived. Everyone assumes it's "the other guy" who is off track. So when people dispute the validity of current revivals, how do you know who is right? In this book Dr. Michael Brown takes a look at current revivals and at the arguments critics are using to question their validity. After examining Scripture, historical accounts of past revivals, and the fruits of the current movements, Dr. Brown comes to a logical conclusion: God's Spirit is moving. *Let No One Deceive You!*
ISBN 1-56043-693-X $10.99p

THE GOD MOCKERS
And Other Messages From the Brownsville Revival
by Stephen Hill.
Hear the truth of God as few men have dared to tell it! In his usual passionate and direct manner, Evangelist Stephen Hill directs people to an uncompromised Christian life of holiness. The messages in this book will burn through every hindrance that keeps you from going further in God!
ISBN 1-56043-691-3 $9.99p

IT'S TIME
by Richard Crisco.
"We say that 'Generation X' does not know what they are searching for in life. But we are wrong. They know what they desire. We, as the Church, are the ones without a revelation of what they need." It is time to stop entertaining our youth with pizza parties and start training an army for God. Find out in this dynamic book how the Brownsville youth have exploded with revival power...affecting the surrounding schools and communities!
ISBN 1-56043-690-5 $9.99p

A TOUCH OF GLORY
by Lindell Cooley.
This book was written for the countless "unknowns" who, like Lindell Cooley, are being plucked from obscurity for a divine work of destiny. Here Lindell, the worship leader of the Brownsville Revival, tells of his own journey from knowing God's hand was upon him to trusting Him. The key to personal revival is a life-changing encounter with the living God. There is no substitute for a touch of His glory.
ISBN 1-56043-689-1 $9.99p

Available at your local Christian bookstore.

Internet: http://www.reapernet.com

Prices subject to change without notice.